Writers at Work

From Sentence to Paragraph

Laurie Blass
Deborah Gordon

CAMBRIDGE UNIVERSITY PRESS
Cambridge, New York, Melbourne, Madrid, Cape Town,
Singapore, São Paulo, Delhi, Mexico City

Cambridge University Press
32 Avenue of the Americas, New York, NY 10013-2473, USA

www.cambridge.org
Information on this title: www.cambridge.org/9780521120302

First published 2010
3rd printng 2012

Printed in Hong Kong, China, by Golden Cup Printing Company Limited

A catalog record for this publication is available from the British Library.

Library of Congress Cataloging in Publication Data
Blass, Laurie, 1952-
Writers at work : from sentence to paragraph / Laurie Blass, Deborah
Gordon.
p. cm.
ISBN 978-0-521-12030-2 (pbk.)
1. English language—Textbooks for foreign speakers. 2. English
language—Rhetoric. 3. English language—Grammar. 4. Report writing. I.
Gordon, Deborah, 1952- II. Title.

PE1128.B537 2010
808'.042—dc22
                                                                    2010011780
ISBN 978-0-521-12030-2 Student's Book
ISBN 978-0-521-12032-6 Teacher's Manual

Art direction, book design, and photo research: Adventure House, NYC
Layout services: Page Designs International, Inc.

Illustration credits: Nancy Lane

Photo credits: page 12: ©Getty Images; page 41: (clockwise from top left) ©Images of Africa
Photobank/Alamy, ©Alamy, ©Chris Mole/Alamy, ©Media Bakery; page 46: ©Getty Images; page 71:
(top to bottom) ©Jeff Greenberg/Alamy, ©The Kobal Collection, ©Everett Collection, ©Itani Images/
Alamy; page 80: ©Everett Collection; page 87: ©Getty Images; page 88 (both) ©Media Bakery; page 90:
(left to right) ©Media Bakery, ©Lisa F. Young/Alamy, ©Media Bakery; page 101: (clockwise from
top left) ©Media Bakery, ©Media Bakery, ©Jeff Morgan/Alamy, ©Payless Images, Inc./Alamy, ©Media
Bakery, ©Media Bakery; page 116: (clockwise from left) ©Media Bakery, ©Media Bakery, ©Inmagine;
page 124: ©Chris Jackson/Getty Images; page 131: (clockwise from top left) ©Maurice Crooks/Alamy,
©Chuck Eckert/Alamy, ©Slick Shoots/Alamy, ©Cephas Picture Library/Alamy, ©Stephen Finn/Alamy,
©Pictures Colour Library/Alamy; page 147: (clockwise from top left) ©Media Bakery, ©Media Bakery,
©KT Spencer/Alamy, ©Media Bakery

Table of Contents

Chapter Contents

Preview the Process

CHAPTER 1 All About Me

* The items in this column refer to the titles of the
information boxes that appear throughout the book.

CHAPTER 2 Home Sweet Home

CHAPTER 3 Work, Play, Sleep

CHAPTER 4 Families

CHAPTER 5 That's Entertainment!

CHAPTER 6 People

CHAPTER 7 Jobs and Careers

CHAPTER 8 Important Life Events

CHAPTER 9 Going Places

CHAPTER 10 In the Future

Appendix

Introduction

THE *WRITERS AT WORK* SERIES

The *Writers at Work* series takes beginning to high intermediate-level writing students through a process approach to writing. The series is intended primarily for adults whose first language is not English, but it may also prove effective for younger writers or for native speakers of English who are developing their competence as independent writers in English.

- *Writers at Work: From Sentence to Paragraph* prepares beginning to high beginning students to write grammatically accurate, topic-related sentences as the basis for an introduction to paragraph writing.

- *Writers at Work: The Paragraph* prepares high beginning to low intermediate students to write well-developed paragraphs using a variety of organization types.

- *Writers at Work: The Short Composition* prepares low intermediate to intermediate-level students to put together several paragraphs to write well-constructed and well-edited short compositions.

- *Writers at Work: The Essay* prepares intermediate to high intermediate students to write fully-developed essays with an introduction, body paragraphs, and a conclusion. Upon completion of this book, students will be ready for more advanced-level academic writing courses.

The approach

Competence in writing comes from knowing *how* to write as much as from knowing *what* to write. That is why the *Writers at Work* books are organized around the process of writing. They teach students about the writing process and then guide them to use it as they write. We believe that once students understand how to use the writing process in writing sentences, paragraphs, short compositions, and essays, they will gain the confidence they need to advance to more complex writing tasks.

In teaching writing to lower-level students, there is always the danger of sacrificing creativity in order to achieve accuracy, or vice versa. The *Writers at Work* books guide students through the writing process in such a way that their final pieces of writing are not only expressive and rich in content, but also clear and accurate.

ABOUT *WRITERS AT WORK: FROM SENTENCE TO PARAGRAPH*

Chapter structure

Each chapter is divided into the following five parts:

I Getting Started

Students are stimulated to think about the topic of the chapter. They learn topic-specific vocabulary and generate ideas through discussion and freewriting. These ideas serve as a springboard for the rest of the writing in the chapter.

II Preparing Your Writing

Students learn and practice new grammar points that they can use in their writing. The contextualized grammar activities and exercises are both at the sentence and paragraph level. At the end of this section, students use the new language they have learned in Sections I and II to write their first drafts.

III Revising Your Writing

Students are introduced to additional lexical sets composed of both words and phrases to help them express and refine their ideas. They also learn ways to express relationships between their ideas. They then apply what they have learned to generate their second drafts.

IV Editing Your Writing

Students are introduced to the mechanics of writing such as capitalization, punctuation, and spelling. They also learn to proofread their writing for specific grammar points. They then apply what they have learned to generate their final drafts.

V Following Up

Students share their writing with each other. Finally, they fill out a self-assessment form, which allows them to track their progress as writers throughout the course.

Key features

- The book begins with an introductory section, "Preview the Process," which introduces students to the writing process, including teaching them how to freewrite, draft, revise, and edit. It also serves to familiarize the students with how the chapters in the book are structured.

- The ten chapters of the book are thematic, each one dealing with a topic of personal interest. All of the activities and exercises in a chapter relate to the theme. Students study topic vocabulary that they can use in their own writing on the theme.

- Sample sentences and paragraphs are presented for students to interact with and edit in preparation for working on their own writing. A major goal of the text is to help students to become more proficient at revising and editing their own writing.

- Instruction is given on how to write clear, grammatically accurate sentences. Strategies are also presented for combining ideas and connecting sentences to show a variety of logical relationships. Later chapters focus on organizing sentences into coherent paragraphs.

- Student interaction is important in *Writers at Work: From Sentence to Paragraph*. Throughout the book, students are carefully guided to help each other write more clearly and think more critically about writing. Collaborative tasks and peer feedback activities in the text make learning to write manageable and enjoyable.

- "Sharing Your Writing" activities at the end of each chapter engage students in sharing their final drafts.

- "Check Your Progress," a self-assessment activity at the end of each chapter, helps students reflect on what they have learned in this and in previous chapters.

A FINAL NOTE

Writers at Work: From Sentence to Paragraph achieves the elusive goal of getting beginning-level students to benefit from a writing process approach. This is done through scaffolding the writing process with a strong emphasis on language development in the first steps of the process. This language development serves as a foundation for writing coherent and cohesive topic-related sentences in the first seven chapters, and paragraphs in the final three chapters.

Acknowledgements

We would like to thank all the people who helped us make *Writers at Work: From Sentence to Paragraph* possible.

First and foremost, we'd like to thank the editorial staff at Cambridge University Press. We would especially like to thank Bernard Seal, senior commissioning editor, for his vision in believing that a low-level writing process book was not an anomaly, and for his firm but instructive guidance at all steps of the process. We especially appreciate his patience and his willingness to listen to us when we weren't all of the same mind about something.

Writers at Work: From Sentence to Paragraph wouldn't be the book it is without our editor, Caitlin Mara. Caitlin's meticulous eye for detail was invaluable. We especially appreciated Caitlin's ability to see solutions at times when we hit a wall. Her clear feedback coupled with her sense of humor made our process easy and pleasurable.

Many thanks also go to Susan Ryan for getting us started on this project in the first place.

Thanks are also due to all the low-level students we have taught over the years in various places, but especially to the students at Santa Barbara City College, Santa Barbara, CA, and The International Rescue Committee, San Diego, CA, for keeping us grounded and aware of what students at this level can do, what their needs are, and what they most benefit from.

We would also like to thank the following reviewers for their valuable comments and insights: Donna Biscay, Shoreline Community College; Tim Brotherton, Clarkston Campus, Georgia Perimeter College; Mark F. Koenig, Daejin University; Jennie Longmire, Sierra Community College; Steve McIsaac, University of Southern California; Pinar Ozdemir, Bilgi University.

Many thanks also go to Don Williams, the compositor, and to the designers at Adventure House for their care and hard work.

Finally, much heartfelt appreciation to our families for their encouragement and unfailing support.

Preview the Process

This section previews the different steps of the writing process. It also shows you what you learn and do in each chapter of this book.

A Learn new words

LEARNING NEW WORDS

It's a good idea to study words and phrases about a topic before you write. This helps you get ideas for your writing.

In this book, you study a list of words and phrases about a topic before you start to write. This list is called the *Vocabulary Pool*. You can use these words and phrases in your sentences.

Practice **1**

Look at the *Vocabulary Pool* below. A student checked (✓) the words she knows and highlighted the words that she doesn't know. Study the *Vocabulary Pool* and then answer the questions below with a partner.

VOCABULARY POOL

Parts of Speech	Sentence Parts	Writing Terms	Mechanics
✓ noun	subject	freewrite	punctuation
✓ verb	object	✓ first draft	✓ capital letter
✓ adjective	connecting word	✓ second draft	comma
✓ adverb		revise	✓ period
preposition		edit	✓ spelling

1 How many words did the student check (✓)? _____

2 How many words did the student highlight? _____

3 Which words from the *Vocabulary Pool* do you and your partner know? Check (✓) these words.

4 Which words from the *Vocabulary Pool* are you both unsure about? Highlight these words.

5 With your partner, talk about the meaning of the words in the *Vocabulary Pool*.

B Freewrite

FREEWRITING

Freewriting is a way to help you get ideas for your writing. Freewriting is called "free" because you write without thinking about the rules. When you freewrite, you don't worry about grammar, spelling, punctuation, or writing in complete sentences. You just think about your ideas. You don't worry if they are good ideas or bad ideas.

When you freewrite, you work quickly. You keep your pen or pencil on the paper. You don't stop to think. If you can't think of any ideas, you keep writing anyway. You can write, "I don't have any more ideas," or something similar. After you write that, more ideas may come to mind.

When you freewrite, you can write words, phrases, or sentences. When you make a mistake or want to change your ideas, you don't erase. That takes too much time. Just cross out your mistake and keep writing. It doesn't matter how messy or neat your freewrite is. It's just for you.

In this book, you freewrite before you write your first draft. Remember, a freewrite is not a first draft. It is only a list of ideas. Some of the ideas are useful and some aren't.

Practice 2

Read this student's freewrite about the problems she has when she writes in English. Then answer the questions with a partner.

1 How many places did the student cross out words?

_____

2 Find four problems the student says she has. Underline them.

3 Highlight any of the student's problems that you have, too.

4 With your partner, talk about other writing problems that you have.

> *I very slow. make lots ~~wrong~~ mistake. dont know to say. ideas ~~no good~~ not many. ~~dont hav idea dont hav idea dont hav i~~ need more grammr and words. dont know difrence nouns verbs adjectives adverbs prepositions. I dont hav idea Do not know many words What subject and object? I know periods + puntuation but no understnd commas. writing hard. ~~no like.~~ freewriting first time. i like it easy*

Your turn ↫

Freewrite about *your* writing problems. Write everything that comes to mind, and don't worry about grammar or spelling. You can look back at the *Vocabulary Pool* to help you. Don't take your pen or pencil off the paper. Just keep writing. If you can't think of anything to write, just write, "I can't think of anything to write." Remember, you don't have to show your freewrite to anyone.

STARTING TO WRITE

A Learn grammar

> **LEARNING GRAMMAR**
>
> You need to know how to write correct sentences so your readers can understand your ideas. To do this, you need to learn grammar. Grammar helps you to express your ideas clearly.
>
> In this book, you learn the grammar you need to write correct sentences. You practice the grammar in practice exercises. Then you use the grammar in your own writing.

Practice 3

Look at this practice exercise on subjects and verbs. The instructions told students to circle the subjects and underline the verbs. Look at one student's answers. Are they correct? Explain your answer to a partner.

1 (I) forget grammar.

2 (My sentences) are too short.

3 (Punctuation) is difficult.

4 (Freewriting) gives me ideas.

5 (Correct grammar) makes my writing clear.

6 (My partner and I) know 10 words in the *Vocabulary Pool*.

B Write the first draft

> **WRITING THE FIRST DRAFT**
>
> When you write the first draft, you put your ideas together into sentences.
>
> In this book, you use many things to help you write your first draft.
> • The words and phrases from the *Vocabulary Pool*
> • Some of the ideas from your freewrite
> • The grammar that you are learning

Practice 4

Read a student's first draft on writing problems. Then answer the questions with a partner.

> Writing is hard. my writing have a lot of mistakes. I forget grammar. Like what a subject and what is a object? I dont know about commas and capital letters. I dont have ideas my sentences are to short

1 How many words from the *Vocabulary Pool* on page 2 did the student use? _____

2 How many ideas from the *Freewrite* on page 3 did the student use? _____

3 How many new ideas did the student add? _____

4 How many sentences have a subject and a verb? _____

III REVISING YOUR WRITING

A Revise

REVISING DRAFTS

Revising means improving your ideas and the way that you write them. It is a very important part of the writing process. Every time you revise, you write a new draft. Students often need to write two or three drafts before a piece of writing is ready to give to the teacher.

When you revise, it's a good idea to think about your vocabulary. Try to add new words and phrases to make your writing more interesting. To do this, re-read your first draft and find different ways to express your ideas. You may also think of new ideas to write about.

It is also important to connect your ideas when you revise. This helps the reader understand them. In this book, you learn how to connect your ideas with connecting words, such as *also, and, but,* and *for example.* This is another way to make your writing better.

In this book, you study some new topic vocabulary and some ways to connect your ideas before you write your second draft. Then you make changes on your first draft. Next, you rewrite your draft, and this becomes your second draft. It's good to type your second draft on a computer, if possible.

Practice 5

This student started to revise her first draft. She marked up her first draft with some changes. Read the first draft. With a partner, answer the question below.

> *difficult*   *rules*
>
> Writing is ~~hard~~. my writing have a lot of mistakes. I forget grammar, ~~Like~~
>
> *for example*   *?*   *I also use the wrong verb.*
>
> ^what a subject ~~and~~ what is a object? I dont know ~~about commas and~~
>
> *the rules about punctuation. I have other problems*
>
> ^~~capital letters.~~ I dont have ideas^my sentences are to short
>
>   *and*

Which of the following changes did the student make? Circle your answer(s). Explain your answers to your partner.

a The student changed some words.

b The student changed the order of her sentences.

c The student added sentences.

d The student added connecting words and phrases.

B Give and get feedback

GIVING AND GETTING FEEDBACK

Giving and getting feedback means to work with another student on your writing. When you give feedback, it's important to first say something you like about your partner's draft. You can give suggestions after that. Suggestions need to be positive and helpful.

Example:

    Student A: I like your second sentence about . . . It's interesting. I didn't know
                    that before.

    Student B: Thanks.

    Student A: I have a suggestion. You can use *and* to connect the third and
                    fourth sentences.

    Student B: Good idea. Thanks. Is there anything else?

    Student A: Yes. You can add a sentence at the end.

In this book, you always give feedback to another student. You also always get feedback. Your partner's ideas are just suggestions. Use the suggestions that you like in your second draft. Thinking about feedback helps you improve your writing.

Practice 6

Read the marked up first draft in *Practice 5* again. Then complete the chart and follow the steps below it.

How many words or phrases from the *Vocabulary Pool* did the student use?	
How many connecting words, such as *also*, *and*, *but*, or *for example*, did the student use?	
How many words did the student cross out?	
What do you like about the student's draft? Underline one or two things.	

1 Work with a partner. Tell your partner what you like about this student's writing.
2 Show your partner the chart. Discuss your answers. Do you have any suggestions for this student to use in her second draft?

Practice 7

The student got suggestions from her partner to help her revise her first draft. Read her second draft below. What changes did the student make? Did she make any changes that you suggested in *Practice 6*?

> Writing is difficult for me. my writing have a lot of grammar mistakes. I forget grammar rules. for example what a subject? what is a object? I also use the wrong verb. I dont know the rules about punctuation. I have other problems i dont have a lot of ideas and my sentences are to short

A Focus on mechanics

FOCUSING ON MECHANICS

Mechanics are things like
- punctuation, such as capital letters, commas, and periods
- spelling
- grammar mistakes

In this book, you correct the mechanics on the second draft.

Practice 8

This student edited her second draft. Study the changes that she made. Then answer the questions with a partner.

                                            M   has

Writing is difficult for me. ~~my~~ writing ~~have~~ a lot of grammar mistakes. I

                         F   ,   is   and   an

forget grammar rules. for example what a subject? what is ~~a~~ object? I also

                             don't

use the wrong verb. I ~~dont~~ know the rules about punctuation. I have other

            . I don't   too   .

problems ~~i dont~~ have a lot of ideas and my sentences are ~~to~~ short

---

1 What spelling corrections did this student make?

2 What punctuation corrections did this student make?

3 What grammar corrections did this student make?

B Write the final draft

WRITING THE FINAL DRAFT

After you make all the changes to your second draft, it's time to rewrite it or revise it on your computer again. This is the final draft. It has all of your additions and corrections. It has ideas and suggestions from your classmates. It is clean and neat.

In this book, you write a final draft and share it with your classmates and teacher.

Practice 9

Read the student's freewrite, first draft, second draft, and final draft. With a partner, talk about how each draft is different.

Freewrite

> I very slow. make lots ~~wrong~~ mistake. dont know to say. ideas ~~no good~~ not many. ~~dont hav idea dont hav idea dont hav i~~ need more grammr and words. dont know difrence nouns verbs adjectives adverbs prepositions. I dont hav idea Do not know many words What subject and object? I know periods + puntuation but no understnd commas. writing hard. ~~no like.~~ freewriting first time. i like it easy

First draft

> Writing is hard. my writing have a lot of mistakes. I forget grammar. Like what a subject and what is a object? I dont know about commas and capital letters. I dont have ideas my sentences are to short

Second draft

> Writing is difficult for me. my writing have a lot of grammar mistakes. I forget grammar rules. for example what a subject? what is a object? I also use the wrong verb. I dont know the rules about punctuation. I have other problems i dont have a lot of ideas and my sentences are to short

Final draft

> Writing is difficult for me. My writing has many grammar mistakes. I forget grammar rules. For example, what is a subject and what is an object? I also use the wrong verb. I don't know the rules about punctuation. For example, I make mistakes with commas and capital letters. I have other problems. I don't have a lot of ideas and my sentences are too short.

All About Me

Think about yourself. Who are you? Where are you from? Are you married or single? What are your interests? What are your favorite things?

In this chapter, you write about yourself.

A Useful vocabulary

Follow these steps to study words and phrases to use when you write about yourself.

1 Work with a partner. Talk about the words in the *Vocabulary Pool*. Together, check (✓) the words you both know, and highlight the ones you don't know.

VOCABULARY POOL

Countries	Useful Verbs	Useful Nouns	Useful Adjectives	Useful Phrases
Brazil	go to	city	favorite	My name is . . .
Canada	like	country	married	I'm from . . .
China	live	food	single	I'm interested in . . .
Japan	love	name		I'm ___ years old.
Mexico	play	nickname		My favorite ___
Saudi Arabia	speak	school		is . . .
Turkey	study	student		I'm good at . . .
the United States	work	teacher		

2 Change partners. Look at your new partner's highlighted words. Explain them to your partner if you can.

3 Walk around the room. Talk to other students. Learn the name of each person that you talk to and which country they come from. Learn one special thing about each person, too. You can ask these questions:

- What's your name?
- Where are you from?
- What's your favorite sport / food / type of music . . . ?

B Vocabulary in context

Follow these steps to use and read words and phrases from the *Vocabulary Pool*.

- Work with a partner. Look at the pictures. Talk about any differences you can see.
- Read about Marisol Cruz. Check (✓) the picture that matches her description.
- Underline the words that helped you find the answer.

My name is Marisol Cruz. My nickname is Mari. I'm from Mexico. I'm 28 years old. I'm married. My husband and I live in Austin, Texas. I'm a student at Austin City College. I study English. I'm not good at cooking, but I love food. I like food from different countries. I love Chinese food and Japanese food. I also like music. I love Brazilian music. My favorite singer is Daniela Mercury. I like sports, too. I play tennis and soccer.

C Get ideas

Follow these steps to get ideas to write about yourself.

1 Look at the topics below. Check (✓) the ones you can use to write about yourself.

☐ country   ☐ work   ☐ school   ☐ age   ☐ family

☐ sports   ☐ interests   ☐ favorite food   ☐ favorite music

2 Work with a partner. Tell your partner about yourself. Use the topics above to help you.

D Freewrite

Freewrite about yourself. Your teacher will tell you when to start and stop writing. To find out how to do freewriting, see the box *Freewriting* on page 3.

A Learn about the simple present of *be*

SIMPLE PRESENT OF BE

You can use the simple present of *be* to talk about yourself and other people.

Subject	*Be*	
I	am	
You	are	a student.
He, She, It	is	
We	are	
You (pl.)	are	students.
They	are	

- You can use *be* with nouns.

  I **am** a student.

- You can use *be* with adjectives.

  He **is** single.

- You can use *be* + *from* to talk about where you are from.

  I **am from** Canada.

  Reza **is from** Iran.

  My husband and I **are from** New York.

Note: To make the negative, put *not* after *be*.

  I **am not** a student. I am a teacher.

  He **is not** single. He is married.

  They **are not** from Iran. They are from New York.

Practice 1

Complete the sentences with the correct form of *be*.

The students in our class _____ from many different places. I _____ from
                           (1)   (2)

Brazil. Clara _____ from Brazil, too. We _____ both from Rio. Asad and
             (3)   (4)

Azziza _____ from Saudi Arabia. Sachi _____ from Japan. Raul, Claudia, and
       (5)   (6)

Betty _____ from Mexico. Ahmed _____ from Turkey. Li-Hua _____ a new
      (7)   (8)   (9)

student. She _____ from China. Rob _____ our teacher. He _____ not from
           (10)   (11)   (12)

the United States. He _____ from Canada. We _____ from all over the world!
                (13)   (14)

Practice 2

Add the correct form of *be* to make complete sentences. Remember to add *from* to talk about places.

1 Mari / Japan *Mari is from Japan.*

2 Jack and Lucy / not / teachers _____

3 I / interested in / Brazilian music _____

4 We / good at / sports _____

5 They / not / China _____

6 My favorite food / Chinese _____

7 My name / Claudia _____

8 Diego / Colombia _____

9 We / married _____

B Learn more about the simple present of *be*

CONTRACTIONS WITH BE

We often use contractions with *be*. We use contractions in informal writing to describe ourselves and other people.

I**'m** single.

He**'s** interested in Brazilian music.

They**'re** from Canada.

We use contractions with negative sentences, too.

I**'m not** single.

He **isn't** interested in Brazilian music.

They **aren't** from Canada.

Subject	*Be*	Contractions	Negative Contractions
I	am	I'm	I'm not
You	are	You're	You're not *or* You aren't
He	is	He's	He's not *or* He isn't
She	is	She's	She's not *or* She isn't
It	is	It's	It's not *or* It isn't
We	are	We're	We're not *or* We aren't
They	are	They're	They're not *or* They aren't

Practice 3

Change the forms of *be* to contractions.

> ¹I ~~am~~ *I'm* Francisco. ²I am from Colombia. ³I have a nickname. ⁴It is Franco.
> ⁵I live in Los Angeles now. ⁶I live with my family. ⁷My sister and I go to school.
> ⁸We are students at L.A. City College. ⁹I am not married. ¹⁰I am still single.
> ¹¹I am interested in sports. ¹²I am not good at tennis. ¹³It is too hard. ¹⁴I am
> good at soccer. ¹⁵It is a lot of fun.

Practice 4

Change each sentence to a negative. Then write another sentence with the information in the parentheses. Use contractions.

1 He is from <u>China</u>.   (Taiwan)
He isn't from China. He's from Taiwan.

2 She is a <u>teacher</u>.   (student)

3 I am from <u>New York</u>.   (San Francisco)

4 They are from <u>El Salvador</u>.   (Costa Rica)

5 He is <u>single</u>.   (married)

6 She is from <u>Poland</u>.   (Bulgaria)

7 We are good at <u>tennis</u>.   (soccer)

8 You are interested in <u>music</u>.   (sports)

C Write the first draft

Now it's time to write the first draft. Write about yourself. Use your freewrite and your ideas and language from Sections I and II to help you. You can add any other ideas that come to mind.

▐▐▐ REVISING YOUR WRITING

A Expand your vocabulary

> ### NATIONALITY WORDS
>
> Countries are nouns. Nationalities are adjectives. Nationality adjectives are often similar to the country name. Many end in *-ian*, *-an*, *-n*, *-ese*, *-i*, and *-ish*.
>
> Canadian, Korean, Tunisian, Japanese, Iraqi, English
>
> Some nationality words look very different from the country word.
>
> Spanish (Spain), Thai (Thailand), Filipino (the Philippines)
>
> Most nationality words are also the names of the languages from that country.
>
> Cam is from Vietnam. She's Vietnamese. She speaks Vietnamese.
>
> For more nationality words, see Appendix A on page 161.

Practice 5

Look at the pictures. Do you know which countries the foods are from? Discuss with a partner. Then complete the sentences below with nationality words from the box.

sushi   kebabs   hamburger   fish and chips   tacos   egg rolls

American	Chinese	English	Japanese	Egyptian	Mexican

1 My favorite food is ___*Japanese*___ food. I love sushi.

2 I love _____ food. I like fish and chips a lot.

3 My brother loves hamburgers. They're _____.

4 I'm good at cooking _____ food. My family loves my tacos.

5 My wife is _____. She makes kebabs a lot.

6 Rang's favorite food is _____. She loves egg rolls.

Your turn ↩

Look at your first draft. Did you write any sentences using nationality words? On your draft, add sentences with nationality words. Remember to mark where these sentences go.

B Connect your ideas

Practice 6

Write sentences with the words in parentheses. Use *and*.

1 I work at (the Holiday Inn) (the Ramada)

I work at the Holiday Inn and the Ramada.

2 I live with (my mother) (my father)

_____

3 I'm a student at (L.A. City College) (Evans Adult School)

_____

4 I live with (my wife) (my two children)

_____

5 I speak (Spanish) (Portuguese)

_____

6 I'm good at (piano) (guitar)

_____

7 I like (tennis) (soccer)

_____

8 I take (an English class) (a computer class)

_____

Your turn ↶

Look at your first draft. Did you use *and* in any sentences? On your draft, write one or more *and* sentences. Remember to mark where these sentences go.

C Give and get feedback

Work with a partner. Follow these steps to give and get feedback.

1 Show your partner your first draft with any sentences you added to it.

2 Exchange books. Answer the questions in the chart below about your partner's piece of writing.

	Your Partner's Writing
How many words or phrases from the *Vocabulary Pool* did your partner use?	
How many sentences have a form of *be*?	
How many nationality words did your partner use?	
How many sentences have *and*?	

3 What do you like about your partner's piece of writing? Underline one or two parts. Tell your partner.

4 Show your partner the chart. Discuss your answers. Do you have any suggestions for your partner?

5 Return your partner's book.

D Write the second draft

Follow these steps to write the second draft.

1 Look at the chart your partner completed for your first draft. Think about what your partner said. Did your partner give you any ideas that you can use? For example, can you add any more sentences with nationality words?

2 Rewrite your draft with the changes.

A Focus on mechanics

USING CAPITAL LETTERS AND PERIODS

Use capital letters in the following places.

- For the pronoun *I*

    I am from Turkey.

- For the first letter of the first word of all sentences

    They work in a school.

- For the first letter of names, places, languages, and nationalities

    My name is **A**bbas. I am from **M**orocco. I speak **A**rabic and **F**rench.

Put a period at the end of sentences that are not questions.

    My name is Abbas**.** I am Moroccan**.**

For more rules about capital letters, see Appendix B on page 162.

Practice **7**

Read the sentences. Some capital letters and periods are missing. Find the mistakes and fix them.

> ~~m~~y name is fernando I'm mexican I'm from chiapas i go to holyoke
> *M*
>
> Community College I work at dash, a store in the mall i also work at the
>
> hospital I live in Northampton now. I live with another student, Thiago Thiago
>
> is a difficult name for americans. his nickname is james James is brazilian He's
>
> from são Paolo he speaks portuguese and english i speak spanish and english.
>
> i'm good at sports my favorite sports are basketball and baseball

Your turn ⟿

Look at your second draft. Check your use of capital letters. Make sure every sentence ends with a period.

B Check for common mistakes

> **MISSING BE VERBS**
>
> Many students forget to use the verb *be*.
>
> | Wrong | Right |
> |---|---|
> | I Korean. | I'm Korean. |
> | He a student. | He's a student. |

Practice 8

Read the description. Find nine more places where *be* is missing. Write the correct form of *be* in the correct place.

> ¹My name ᵢₛ^ Roberta Sanchez. ²I'm Costa Rican. ³I from Monteverde. ⁴I married. ⁵My husband Mexican. ⁶We students at Western State University. ⁷I a nurse. ⁸My husband a nurse, too. ⁹I interested in lots of things. ¹⁰We in a very good rock band! ¹¹My favorite type of music rock music.

C Edit your writing

Use the *Editing Checklist* below to edit your sentences. Look for only one kind of mistake each time you read your sentences. For example, the first time you read your sentences, ask yourself, "Does every sentence start with a capital letter?"

> ## EDITING CHECKLIST ☑
>
> ☐ **1** Does every sentence start with a capital letter?
>
> ☐ **2** Does every sentence end with a period?
>
> ☐ **3** Did you use *be* verbs correctly?
>
> ☐ **4** Are the nationality words correct?

D Write the final draft

Make all your changes on your second draft. Remember to mark where the changes go. Rewrite the draft. Make any changes that you need.

A Share your writing

Follow these steps to share your writing.

1 Find a picture to go with your writing. Some picture ideas are: a picture of you or of you and your family, a picture of your home, a map of your country, a picture of a famous place in your country, or a picture of something important that comes from your country. Don't put your name on your picture.

2 Put your picture on the wall or on a table. Then give your teacher your writing. Your teacher will give you another student's piece of writing.

3 Read the writing your teacher gives you. Then find the picture that matches the writing. Stand next to the matching picture.

B Check your progress

After you get your writing back from your teacher, complete the *Progress Check* below.

PROGRESS CHECK

Date: _____

New vocabulary I used: _____

_____

_____

New grammar I used: _____

_____

Connecting words I used: _____

Mechanics I learned: _____

Things I need to remember the next time I write: _____

_____

Home Sweet Home

Some people live in an apartment. Some people live in a house. Some people live in one room. Where do you live? Think about your home. How many rooms are there? What is in each room?

In this chapter, you write about homes and what is in them.

A Useful vocabulary

Follow these steps to study words and phrases to use when you write about homes.

1 Work with a partner. Talk about the words in the *Vocabulary Pool*. Together, check (✓) the words you both know, and highlight the ones you don't know.

VOCABULARY POOL

apartment	counter	mirror
apartment building	curtains	nightstand
bathroom	desk	refrigerator
bathtub	dining room	room
bed	dishwasher	rug
bedroom	dresser	shelf
blinds	dryer	shower
bookcase	fireplace	sink
bookshelf	hall	stove
carpet	home	table
chair	house	toilet
closet	kitchen	towel racks
coffee table	laundry room	washing machine
couch	living room	yard

2 Change partners. Look at your new partner's highlighted words. Explain them to your partner if you can.

3 With your partner, complete the chart with words from the *Vocabulary Pool*. Some words can go into more than one room.

Living Room	Dining Room	Kitchen	Bedroom	Bathroom
couch	table	table	mirror	towel racks mirror

4 Tell your partner about a room you know well.

B Vocabulary in context

Follow these steps to use and read words and phrases from the *Vocabulary Pool*.

- Work with a partner. Look at the pictures. Talk about the things in each picture.
- Read about each home. Now find the picture that matches each description. Write the letter on the line.
- Reread the descriptions. Underline the words that helped you find the answer.

_____ 1   My dream home is a house in a nice neighborhood. The house has a living room, a dining room, a kitchen, two bathrooms, and three bedrooms. All the rooms are very big and bright. The rooms have comfortable furniture. There are trees in the yard.

_____ 2   My place is very small. There are two beds. There are two desks and two chairs. There is no closet. Clothes and shoes are everywhere. There are books and papers on the desks. There is one bookshelf. There are some DVDs and books on the bookshelf. The bookshelf is behind an old dresser.

_____ 3   The Greens' home is very nice. For example, the living room has a couch, two chairs, a big bookcase, and a coffee table in the middle of the room. There's also a fireplace. There are a lot of books and pictures in the bookcase. There are flowers on the coffee table.

_____ 4   Tony and Lynn's building isn't very nice. The apartments are tiny. They only have two rooms. The apartments are also very dark. There is only one window in each room. The building isn't in a very nice neighborhood. It's on a noisy street with a lot of traffic, but it's near school.

C Get ideas

Follow these steps to get ideas to write about homes.

1 Look at this drawing of a small apartment. Answer the questions that follow.

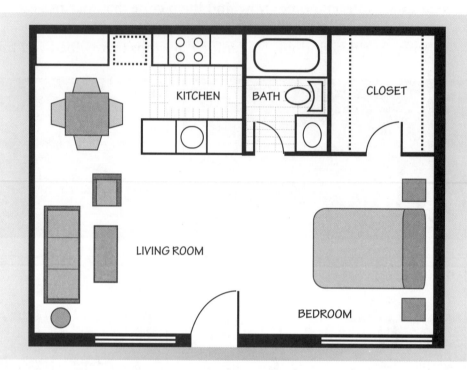

- What's in the bathroom?
- What's in the kitchen?
- What's in the living room?
- What's in the bedroom?

2 On a separate piece of paper, draw two rooms that you know well. Draw circles and squares for the things in the room. Write the names of each thing on the circles and squares.

3 Work with a partner. Tell each other about your rooms.

4 Did your partner use any words from the *Vocabulary Pool* that you can use? Add them to your drawings.

D Freewrite

Freewrite about the topics below. For each topic, your teacher will tell you when to start and stop writing. Write everything that you think of, and don't worry about grammar or spelling. You can write words, phrases, and sentences. Don't stop to erase anything. Just keep writing.

Freewrite 1 Your home

Freewrite 2 Your dream home

A Learn about *there is* / *there are*

USING THERE IS / THERE ARE

We often use *there is* (*there's*) and *there are* to talk about things that are in places.

* Use *there is* when the noun after it is singular.

   There is a couch in the living room.

* Use *there are* when the noun after it is plural.

   There are two beds in the bedroom.

* In sentences with more than one noun, the first noun that follows *there is* or *there are* tells you which form of *be* to use.

   There is a couch and chairs in the living room.

   There are two beds and a dresser in the bedroom.

* Use *no* after the verb to make the sentence negative.

   There's no fireplace.

   There are no chairs.

Note: *There is* and *there are* usually come at the beginning of a sentence.

Practice 1

Read the following sentences. Circle *is* or *are*.

In my dream house, there (is) / are a big living room. There is / are lots
(1)   (2)
of windows, and there is / are a big fireplace. There is / are a big TV over the
(3)   (4)
fireplace. There is / are a soft couch and chairs in front of the fireplace, and
(5)
there is / are tall bookshelves to the right and to the left of the fireplace. There
(6)
is / are lots of books on the bookshelves. There is / are beautiful floors, and
(7)   (8)
there is / are a beautiful rug on the floor. There is / are a lot of windows. There
(9)   (10)
is / are no curtains on the windows, so there is / are a nice view of the yard.
(11)   (12)
The yard is very beautiful. There is / are lots of flowers in the yard.
(13)

Practice **2**

Read about American dormitories. Then answer the following questions. Use *there is* or *there are* in your answers.

Many American college students live in dormitories. For example, at Marin University, a typical dorm room has two beds and two dressers. There are also two closets. There's a sink and two towel racks. There's a mirror, too. There are two desks and two chairs. There are no couches. There are lots of shelves for textbooks and televisions. There's one window in each room. There are no blinds on the windows. There's a kitchen on the first floor. In the kitchen, there's a stove and two large sinks. There are no tables or chairs in the kitchen.

1 How many closets are there in each dorm room?

There are two closets.

2 Are there couches in the dorm rooms?

_____

3 Are there any windows?

_____

4 What's on the first floor?

_____

5 What's in the kitchen?

_____

6 Why is it difficult to eat a meal in the kitchen?

_____

B Learn about *has* / *have*

USING HAS / HAVE

You can also use *has* or *have* to talk about the number of rooms in a home, or to describe what is in a room.

- Use *has* after singular noun subjects

    My apartment **has** two bedrooms and one bathroom.

- Use *have* after plural noun subjects

    They **have** a beautiful home near the city.

Practice 3

Match the two parts of the sentences. Write the letter in the blank.

__d__	1 My kitchen	a have two beds.
_____	2 These bathrooms	b has a gray carpet.
_____	3 The front door	c have no shelves.
_____	4 Both bedrooms	d has a big refrigerator and a stove.
_____	5 The yard	e has apartments and houses.
_____	6 My sister and I	f have four apartments in them.
_____	7 The hall	g have big bathtubs.
_____	8 These buildings	h has a lot of trees.
_____	9 Our neighborhood	i has big black numbers on it.
_____	10 The closets	j have one window in our bedroom.

Practice 4

Read the sentences. Circle the subjects in the numbered sentences. Draw an arrow from the subject to *has* or *have*. Circle *has* or *have*.

I live in an apartment building on Stratford Street in Hillspoint, Connecticut. There are many apartment buildings on my street. My building (has) / have 12 (1) apartments and a big yard. All of the apartments has / have three rooms. In (2) my apartment, there's one bedroom, one living room, and a kitchen. There's no dining room. There's a bathroom, too. My bedroom has / have two beds. The (3) living room has / have two chairs and a comfortable couch. The living room (4) has / have a dining table in it, too. All of the rooms has / have lots of big (5) (6) windows. The kitchen has / have a great view of the yard. (7)

USING HAS / HAVE AND THERE IS / THERE ARE

It is good to use different types of sentences when you write.

Don't use *there is / there are* all the time. Use *has / have* sometimes.

There's a bathtub in my bathroom. ➔ My bathroom **has** a bathtub.

There are big windows in the bedrooms. ➔ The bedrooms **have** big windows.

Remember: The verb *be* in *there is / there are* agrees with the noun that comes right after it. The verb *has / have* agrees with the subject that comes before it.

There are no desks in the bedrooms. ➔ The bedrooms have no desks.

Practice 5

Read the *a* sentences. Then complete the *b* sentences. Use *has* or *have*.

1 a There are three windows in the living room.

   b The living room *has three windows* .

2 a There's a coffee table in the living room.

   b The living room _____ .

3 a In both bathrooms, there's a bathtub and a shower.

   b Both bathrooms _____ .

4 a There are blue walls in the living room and the kitchen.

   b The living room and kitchen _____ .

5 a There's a mirror on the closet door.

   b The closet door _____ .

6 a There are two nightstands in the bedroom.

   b The bedroom _____ .

7 a There are three apartment buildings in my neighborhood.

   b My neighborhood _____ .

8 a There's a table and chairs in the yard.

   b The yard _____ .

Practice **6**

Read the description of a house. Cross out each mistake and write the correction above it. There are six more mistakes.

> ¹My family lives in a big house in the country. ²There ~~is~~ *are* lots of rooms in this house. ³The house have five bedrooms. ⁴I has five brothers and three sisters. ⁵I share a bedroom with two brothers. ⁶My bedroom has three beds. ⁷There are a dresser and a big closet, too. ⁸There are two desks in my bedroom. ⁹My three sisters has one bedroom, too. ¹⁰The house have a big yard. ¹¹There is a chair in the yard. ¹²There is also a lot of apple trees in the yard.

Practice **7**

Read this description of apartment buildings in New York City. On a separate piece of paper, rewrite the description, and change sentences 1, 3, 5, 7, 9, and 11. In these sentences, use *has / have* instead of *there is* (*there's*) */ there are*.

> ¹There are some very old apartment buildings in New York City. ²There are five or six floors in these buildings. ³There's one apartment on each floor. ⁴There's a very long hall in each apartment. ⁵There's a kitchen and small bathroom in each apartment. ⁶There is a very small refrigerator, sink, and stove in the kitchen. ⁷There's no oven in the kitchen. ⁸There is a bathtub and a shower in the bathroom. ⁹There are one or two bedrooms in these apartments. ¹⁰There is no living room. ¹¹There's no dining room in these apartments, either.

Example: *New York City has some very old apartment buildings.*

C Write the first draft

Now it's time to write the first draft of two pieces of writing. Use your freewrites and your ideas and language from Sections I and II to help you. You can also add any other ideas that come to mind.

Writing 1 Write a first draft about your home.

Writing 2 Write a first draft about your dream home.

A Expand your vocabulary

PREPOSITIONS OF PLACE

You can use prepositions of place to talk about where things are. Look at these pictures to see some common prepositions.

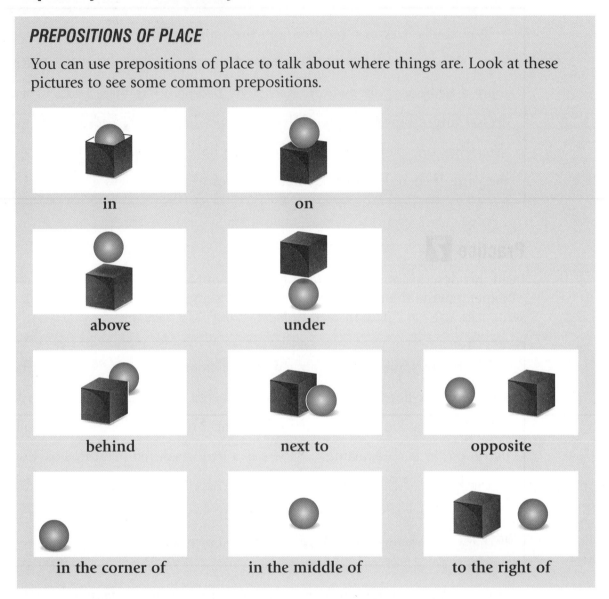

in	on
above	under

behind	next to	opposite
in the corner of	in the middle of	to the right of

Practice 8

Read the sentences below. On a separate piece of paper, draw each room.

1 Draw a kitchen. The kitchen has a sink. There is a window above the sink. There is a stove next to the sink. There is a pot on the stove.

2 Draw a living room. The living room has a couch. There is a coffee table in the middle of the room with a vase on it. There are flowers in the vase. There is a TV in the corner of the room.

3 Draw a bathroom. The bathroom has a bathtub. There is a window to the right of the bathtub. There is a shelf under the window. There is a door opposite the window. There are more shelves behind the door.

Practice 9

Look at the picture. Complete the sentences. Then write the number of the sentence in the correct place in the picture.

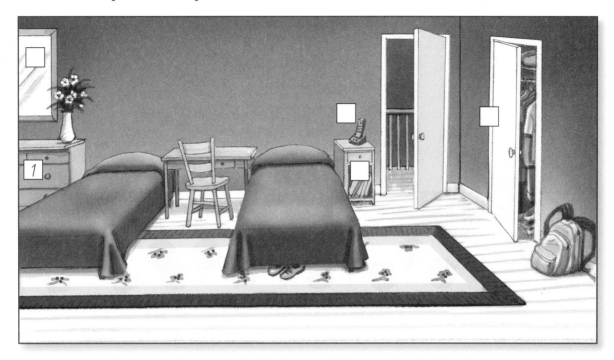

1 ___The dresser___ is to the left of the beds.

2 _____ is above the dresser.

3 _____ is next to the door to the hall.

4 _____ is to the right of the beds.

5 _____ is on the nightstand.

Practice 10

Look at the picture in *Practice 9*. Fill in the blanks with the prepositions from the box *Prepositions of Place* on page 32.

1 The flowers are _____ the dresser.

2 The rug is _____ the room.

3 The desk is _____ the beds.

4 The shoes are _____ the bed.

5 The backpack is _____ of the closet.

Your turn ↩

Look at your first draft of Writing 1 and Writing 2. On each draft, add sentences describing the locations of the rooms and the things in the rooms. Remember to mark where these sentences go.

B Connect your ideas

Practice 11

Rewrite the second sentence in each pair. Use the word in parentheses.

1 Asha's bedroom is big. It's very comfortable.   (too)

It's very comfortable, too.

2 The room has two beds. There's a dresser with a mirror.   (also)

_____

3 Asha's bedroom has a desk. There's a shelf.   (too)

_____

4 There's a computer on the desk. The desk has a big TV on it.   (also)

_____

5 There are lots of books on the shelf. The dresser has books on it.   (too)

_____

6 Asha's windows have curtains. There are blinds on the windows.   (also)

_____

7 There's a chair in the corner. There's a chair at the desk.   (too)

_____

8 There's a picture in the middle of one wall. There's a picture behind the bed.   (also)

_____

Your turn ↶

Look at your first draft of Writing 1 and Writing 2. On each draft, add sentences with *too* and *also*. Remember to mark where these sentences go.

C Give and get feedback

Work with a partner. Follow these steps to give and get feedback.

1 Show your partner your first draft of Writing 1 and Writing 2 with the sentences you added to them.

2 Exchange books. Answer the questions in the chart below about your partner's piece of writing.

	Writing 1	Writing 2
How many words from the *Vocabulary Pool* did your partner use?		
How many sentences use *there is / there are*?		
How many sentences use *has / have*?		
How many sentences use prepositions of place?		
How many sentences use *too* or *also*?		

3 What do you like about each of your partner's pieces of writing? Underline two or three parts. Tell your partner.

4 Show your partner the chart. Discuss your answers. Do you have any suggestions for your partner?

5 Return your partner's book.

D Write the second draft

Follow these steps to write the second draft.

1 Look at the chart your partner completed for your first draft of Writing 1 and Writing 2. Think about what your partner said. Did your partner give you any ideas that you can use? For example, can you add any more sentences with prepositions of place?

2 Look at the *Progress Check* on page 22 of Chapter 1. Use it to help you revise your first draft of Writing 1 and Writing 2.

3 Rewrite each draft with the changes.

A Focus on mechanics

USING THE ARTICLES A AND AN

A and *an* mean *one*. *A* or *an* often goes before singular nouns. Don't use *a* or *an* before plural nouns.

- *A* goes before words that start with consonants or consonant sounds.

  b c d f g h j k l m n p q r s t v w x y z

  There's **a** couch in my living room.

  I live in **a** small apartment.

  The laundry room has **a** useful sink.

- *An* goes before words that start with vowels or vowel sounds.

  a e i o u

  I live in **an** apartment.

  Ken lives in **an** old house.

  Seil lives **an** hour away from work.

Practice 12

Read about Raul's apartment. Find eight more mistakes with *a* and *an*. Cross out each mistake and write the correction above it.

> ¹Raul lives in a̶ apartment building in an noisy neighborhood. ²It isn't in an
> very good location. ³It's a hour away from school. ⁴It's also a old building. ⁵The
> apartment is small, but it has a large windows in the living room. ⁶Raul also
> has an nice kitchen. ⁷The kitchen has a long counters and a electric stove.

(correction above sentence 1: "an")

Your turn

Check your use of *a* and *an* in your second draft of Writing 1 and Writing 2.

B Check for common mistakes

CONFUSING THERE IS *AND* THERE ARE

Many students confuse *there is* and *there are*. Remember that the first noun that follows *there is* and *there are* tells you which form of *be* to use.

Look at these corrected mistakes.

~~There are~~ a bathroom and a kitchen.
There's

~~There's~~ three chairs in the living room.
There are

Practice 13

Read about someone's dream home. Find five more mistakes. Cross out each mistake and write the correction above it.

¹My dream home is a small house in the country. ²There ~~are~~ *is* a living room and a dining room. ³There's also two bedrooms. ⁴In the living room, there are a couch and two chairs. ⁵Opposite the couch, there are a fireplace and a bookshelf. ⁶There's two beds and a dresser in one bedroom. ⁷There is a desk and a big chair in the other bedroom. ⁸There are also a sunny kitchen and a big bathroom.

C Edit your writing

Use the *Editing Checklist* below to edit your sentences. Look for only one kind of mistake each time you read your sentences. For example, the first time you read your sentences, ask yourself, "Does every sentence start with a capital letter?"

EDITING CHECKLIST ✓

☐ **1** Does every sentence start with a capital letter?

☐ **2** Does every sentence end with a period?

☐ **3** Are the nouns that follow *there is* singular?

☐ **4** Are the nouns that follow *there are* plural?

☐ **5** Do the subjects and verbs agree in the *has / have* sentences?

☐ **6** Do the nouns have the correct article in front of them?

D Write the final draft

Make all your changes on your second draft of Writing 1 and Writing 2. Remember to mark where the changes go. Rewrite each draft. Make any changes that you need.

V FOLLOWING UP

A Share your writing

Follow these steps to share your writing.

1 Work with a partner. Read your partner's writing about his or her home.
2 Choose one room and draw it.
3 Show your drawing to your partner. Compare your picture with the writing.

B Check your progress

After you get your writing back from your teacher, complete the *Progress Check* below.

PROGRESS CHECK

Date: _____

New vocabulary I used: _____

_____

_____

New grammar I used: _____

_____

Connecting words I used: _____

Mechanics I learned: _____

Things I need to remember the next time I write: _____

_____

Work, Play, Sleep

Think about the things you do every day. What do you do on weekdays? What do you do on weekends? Where do you go? Who do you see?

In this chapter, you write about daily activities.

A Useful vocabulary

Follow these steps to study words and phrases to use when you write about daily activities.

1 Work with a partner. Talk about the words in the *Vocabulary Pool*. Together, check (✓) the words you both know, and highlight the ones you don't know.

VOCABULARY POOL

go { out home hiking running shopping swimming to a café to a restaurant to bed to school to work to the club to the gym to the mall to the movies	do { chores dishes laundry homework housework have/ { breakfast make { lunch dinner get { up dressed together with friends play { games soccer tennis basketball	check e-mail clean the house fall asleep listen to music pay bills sleep in (late) stay up (late) take classes take the bus watch TV work out (at the gym)

2 Change partners. Look at your new partner's highlighted words. Explain them to your partner if you can.

3 With your partner, complete the chart below with the phrases from the *Vocabulary Pool*. Some activities may go into more than one category.

Everyday Chores or Activities	Free Time or Social Activities	Exercise Activities	Work or School Activities
do laundry	listen to music	go to the gym	go to work

4 Circle the activities that you do. Compare with your partner.

B Vocabulary in context

Follow these steps to use and read words and phrases from the *Vocabulary Pool*.

- Work with a partner. Look at the pictures and talk about the activities they show.
- Read about the daily activities of the people in the pictures. Now find the picture that matches the description of their daily activities. Write the letter of the picture on the line.
- Are any descriptions like your daily activities? Tell your partner what is similar and what is different from what you do.

_____ 1   On weekdays, I go home around 5:30 p.m. I check my e-mail and then go out for a walk. After my walk, I make dinner. After dinner, I watch TV. Sometimes I fall asleep in front of the TV. I don't stay up late. I go to bed around 10:30 p.m.

_____ 2   On Saturday evenings, my wife and I relax. We have dinner at home. We cook dinner together. During dinner, we listen to music. After dinner, we often stay home and watch TV. Other times, we get together with our friends. They come to our house and we play games.

_____ 3   Roberto has very busy weekends. On Saturday and Sunday mornings, he gets up around 6:30 a.m. After he gets up, he goes running. He runs for about two hours. In the middle of the morning, he makes a big breakfast. After breakfast, he either does laundry or pays some bills. In the afternoon, Roberto gets together with friends and plays soccer in the park.

_____ 4   On weekdays, children at the Kituri School in Kenya get up at 6:30 a.m. They brush their teeth and then they get dressed. Then they go to the cafeteria and eat breakfast. After breakfast, they go to their classrooms. At noon, they go outside. They eat lunch and play games. In the afternoon, they go back to their classrooms. After school, they do chores and eat dinner. In the early evening, they do homework and read.

C Get ideas

Follow these steps to get ideas to write about daily activities.

1 Think about your week. Complete the chart with your daily activities.

My week			
	Mornings	Afternoons	Evenings
Weekdays			
Weekends			

2 Work with a partner. Talk about your activities. Did your partner include any activities that you do, too? Add them to your chart.

3 Think of a famous person. Imagine what he or she does every day. Complete the chart with your famous person's daily activities.

_____'s week			
	Mornings	Afternoons	Evenings
Weekdays			
Weekends			

D Freewrite

Freewrite about the topics below. For each topic, your teacher will tell you when to start and stop writing. Write everything that you think of, and don't worry about grammar or spelling. You can write words, phrases, and sentences. Don't stop to erase anything. Just keep writing.

Freewrite 1 Your daily activities

Freewrite 2 A famous person's daily activities

A Learn about the simple present

THE SIMPLE PRESENT

Use the simple present to talk about things that people regularly do.

I **play** soccer on Sundays.

We **take** the bus to work.

They **wake up** at 7:00 a.m. every day.

The verb ends in *-s* when we talk about *he, she,* or *it.*

She **plays** soccer on Sundays.

He **takes** the bus to work.

She **wakes up** at 7:00 a.m. every day.

For *he, she, it,* add *-es* to verbs that end in *ch, sh, ss, s, x,* or *z.*

My neighbor **watches** TV all day.

For more rules about adding *-s* or *-es,* see Appendix C on page 163.

Some verbs are irregular. Some common ones are *do, go,* and *have.*

Max **does** his homework after dinner.

He **goes** to the movies Friday nights.

Rita **has** coffee in the mornings.

For more irregular verbs, see Appendix D on page 164.

Practice **1**

Fill in the blanks. Use the verbs below.

check   do   eats   go   play   runs   starts   take   watches   work

1 Marly _____*runs*_____ on the beach on Saturday mornings.

2 Jason and his brother _____ the bus to school.

3 Many of my friends _____ in restaurants.

4 Class _____ at 8:00 a.m.

5 I _____ my e-mail after work.

6 Francisco and Emilio _____ hiking in the mountains.

7 The children _____ the dishes after dinner.

8 My family _____ dinner at around 7:00 p.m.

9 They _____ basketball on Sundays.

10 He _____ TV at night.

Practice 2

Dara Torres is an Olympic swimmer and a mother. Read her schedule and complete the sentences below.

DAILY PLANNER

Morning
6:00 – get up
6:15 – breakfast with Tessa
8:00–10:30 – swim
11:00 – gym with Anne

Afternoon
12:00 – lunch!
1:00–3:00 – workout with Bob
3:00–5:00 – Mommy and Me swim class with Tessa
5:00 – go home

Dara Torres _____(1)_____ at 6 a.m. Then she _____(2)_____ breakfast with her daughter Tessa. At 8 a.m., she _____(3)_____. Then she _____(4)_____ to the gym with Anne. After that, she _____(5)_____ lunch. At 1 p.m., she _____(6)_____ with Bob. At 3 p.m., she _____(7)_____ a class with Tessa. At 5 p.m., she and Tessa _____(8)_____ home.

THE SIMPLE PRESENT – NEGATIVE

To make the negative, use *do / does not* before the base form of the verb. We often use contractions for these forms.

do not → don't

does not → doesn't

- Use *do not / don't* after *I, you, we,* or *they.*
  I **don't get up** early on Saturdays.

- Use *does not / doesn't* after *he, she,* or *it.*
  He **doesn't work** after school.

Practice 3

Read about Antonio's weekend. Complete the sentences with the verbs in parentheses.

On Saturdays, I _____sleep_____ (sleep) late. I _____ (not get up)
                       (1)   (2)
until 10:00 a.m. Then I _____ (eat) breakfast. I _____ (not
                              (3)   (4)
eat) a big breakfast. After breakfast, I _____ (meet) my friend, Oliver.
                                               (5)
Oliver _____ (live) on my street. We _____ (take) English
            (6)   (7)
classes together. Sometimes we _____ (do) our homework together at
                                      (8)
the library. We also _____ (work out) together at the gym. I
                           (9)
_____ (go) to the movies or to a restaurant in the evening with my
     (10)
friends. Oliver _____ (not go) with us because he _____
                      (11)   (12)
(work) on Saturday evenings. On Saturdays, I _____ (stay up) late!
                                                   (13)
Oliver _____ (go) to bed around 10:00 p.m. On Sundays, I
            (14)
_____ (sleep) in. Oliver _____ (get up) early.
     (15)   (16)

Practice 4

Read about Antonio's weekend again. What does he do that Oliver doesn't do? What does Oliver do that Antonio doesn't do? Write five pairs of sentences.

Example: *Antonio goes to the movies. Oliver doesn't go to the movies.*

1 _____

_____

2 _____

_____

3 _____

_____

4 _____

_____

5 _____

_____

B Learn more about the simple present

USING TIME EXPRESSIONS WITH THE SIMPLE PRESENT

We often use time expressions with the simple present. Notice the prepositions in these time expressions.

- *On* + day / *on* + *weekends*
  Lise works **on Wednesdays**.
  Ana sees friends **on weekends**.

- *At* + time of day / *at* + *night*
  I go to school **at 8 a.m.**
  I don't study **at night**.

- *In* + *the* + part of the day
  Lin doesn't study **in the afternoon**.

- *From* + day or time + *to* + day or time
  I go to school **from 8 a.m. to 2 p.m.**

- *After* / *before* + event
  He goes to the library **after school**.
  Marie does homework **before class**.

Practice 5

Read the sentences below. Underline the time expressions. Circle the prepositions in each time expression.

1 Marta gets up late (on) Sundays.

2 My classes are from 9 a.m. to 12 noon.

3 Marc goes to work at the Elite Café after class.

4 He works there from 2 p.m. to 6 p.m.

5 Susanna does homework and reads in the evenings.

6 The children study before dinner.

7 We don't get up early on Saturday mornings.

8 We play soccer on weekends.

9 Yuta goes to bed at 1 a.m. on weeknights.

10 I take English classes at 8 a.m. on Mondays.

Practice 6

Look at Alejandro's schedule for a weekday. Fill in the blanks below with the correct prepositions.

DAILY PLANNER

MONDAY

Morning

7:00 – Get up
8:00 – Eat breakfast
8:30 – Go to school
9:00-12:00 – English classes

Afternoon

12:30 – Eat lunch
1:00 – Take the bus to work
1:30-5:00 – Work at the café
5:30 – Change clothes
6:00 – Go to the gym
7:00-7:30 – Eat dinner, listen to music

1 Alejandro gets up _____ 7:00 a.m.

2 He goes to school _____ breakfast.

3 _____ Mondays, Alejandro takes English classes.

4 He has class _____ 9:00 a.m. _____ 12:00 noon.

5 _____ lunch, Alejandro goes to work.

6 He works _____ the afternoon.

7 _____ 6:00 p.m., he goes to the gym.

8 Alejandro changes his clothes _____ dinner.

9 He eats dinner _____ 7:00 p.m. _____ 7:30 p.m.

10 _____ night, he listens to music.

C Write the first draft

Now it's time to write the first draft of two pieces of writing. Use your freewrites and your ideas and language from Sections I and II to help you. You can also add any other ideas that come to mind.

Writing 1 Write a first draft about your week.

Writing 2 Write a first draft about a famous person's week.

A Expand your vocabulary

> **APPROXIMATE TIME EXPRESSIONS**
>
> You can use approximate (not exact) time expressions to talk about general times of the day.
>
> - Use *about* and *around* with a point in time to make it less exact.
>   I get up **about** 6:00 a.m. on weekdays.
>   Ana makes dinner **around** 7:00 p.m. every day.
>
> - Use *early, in the middle of the,* and *(in the) late* to talk about general times of the day.
>   Wei goes to work **in the middle of the** morning. (For example, around 10:00 a.m.)
>   Bin goes home in the **late** afternoon. (For example, around 5:00 p.m.)
>
> - Use *during* with an event to talk about a period of time.
>   I watch TV **during** dinner.

Practice 7

Complete the sentences with the approximate time phrases below. Use the times in parentheses to help you choose some of your answers. Use each phrase only once.

| about | around | evening | late morning |
| afternoon | during | late afternoon | morning |

> On weekends, I usually get up early. I get up ___*around*___ 8:00. I go for
> (1)
> a run in the _____ (10:00–10:30). Then I eat a big breakfast in
> (2)
> the _____ (11:00–11:30). _____ breakfast, I read the
> (3)   (4)
> newspaper or start my homework. In the _____ (2:00–4:00), I
> (5)
> check my e-mail, listen to music, and go on Facebook. I don't have lunch. In the
> _____ (5:00), I get together with some friends. We usually have
> (6)
> dinner _____ 6:00. At dinner, we make plans for the rest of the
> (7)
> _____ (8:00–12:00).
> (8)

Your turn

Look at your first draft of Writing 1 and Writing 2. On each draft, add sentences with approximate time expressions. Remember to mark where these sentences go.

B Connect your ideas

Practice 8

Combine the sentences below with *or*.

1 Claudia goes to the gym on Thursdays. Claudia runs in the park on Thursdays.
Claudia goes to the gym or runs in the park on Thursdays.

2 Raffi buys lunch on weekdays. Raffi brings food from home on weekdays.
_____

3 Wei takes the bus to school. Wei takes the train to school.
_____

4 On Saturdays, Marta goes food shopping. On Saturdays, Marta goes to the gym.
_____

5 In the evenings, we sometimes go dancing at a club. In the evenings, we sometimes go out for a meal at a nice restaurant.
_____

6 The students check their e-mail after school. The students text their friends after school.
_____

7 On Sundays, I sleep in. On Sundays, I get up early and do chores.
_____

Practice 9

Read about Rachel's children. Then answer the questions below. Use *or* in your answers. Try to use *either . . . or* in some sentences, too.

I have three children, Robbie, Michael, and Dani. They are very busy on Saturdays. Robbie plays basketball two Saturdays a month. He plays soccer on the other two Saturdays. Sometimes he comes home after the soccer game. Other times, he goes to his friend John's house after the game. Some days, he takes the bus home from John's. Some days, he walks home. Michael takes art classes three Saturdays a month. He goes swimming on the last Saturday of the month. Dani works at the mall on some Saturday mornings. Sometimes she stays at the mall after work. She goes shopping with friends. On other Saturdays, she goes to the movies after work. Sometimes Dani doesn't work on Saturday mornings. On those mornings, she goes to the gym.

1 What does Robbie play on Saturdays?

Robbie plays either basketball or soccer on Saturdays.

2 What does Robbie do after the soccer game?

_____

3 How does Robbie get home from John's house?

_____

4 What does Michael do on Saturdays?

_____

5 What does Dani do on Saturday mornings?

_____

6 What does Dani do after work?

_____

Your turn 〰

Look at your first draft of Writing 1 and Writing 2. Are there any ideas that you can combine with *or* or *either . . . or*? On each draft, add sentences with *or* or *either . . . or*. Remember to mark where these sentences go.

C Give and get feedback

Work with a partner. Follow these steps to give and get feedback.

1 Show your partner your first draft of Writing 1 and Writing 2 with the sentences you added to them.

2 Exchange books. Answer the questions in the chart below about your partner's first drafts.

	Writing 1	Writing 2
How many words or phrases from the *Vocabulary Pool* did your partner use?		
How many sentences are in the simple present?		
How many negative sentences did your partner use?		
How many time expressions did your partner use?		
How many approximate time expressions did your partner use?		
How many sentences have *or* or *either . . . or* in your partner's descriptions?		

3 What do you like about each of your partner's pieces of writing? Underline two or three parts. Tell your partner.

4 Show your partner the chart. Discuss your answers. Do you have any suggestions for your partner?

5 Return your partner's book.

D Write the second draft

Follow these steps to write the second draft.

1 Look at the chart your partner completed for your first draft of Writing 1 and Writing 2. Think about what your partner said. Did your partner give you any ideas you can use? For example, can you add any more sentences with time expressions?

2 Look at the *Progress Check* on page 38 of Chapter 2. Use it to help you revise your first draft of Writing 1 and Writing 2.

3 Rewrite each draft with the changes.

A Focus on mechanics

TIME EXPRESSIONS AT THE BEGINNING OF THE SENTENCE

You can use some time expressions at the beginning of a sentence. This adds variety to your sentences. Use a comma when the time expression comes at the beginning of the sentence.

Bernardo does chores **in the morning**. ➜ **In the morning,** Bernardo does chores.

Jin plays soccer **on weekends**. ➜ **On weekends,** Jin plays soccer.

Practice 10

Put these words in the right order. If the time expression begins with a capital letter, put it at the beginning of the sentence and use a comma.

1 at the City Café / On weekends / Tyler works
On weekends, Tyler works at the City Café.

2 after work / goes to the gym / My brother

_____

3 makes a big breakfast / on Sundays / Rafael

_____

4 Susanna / From 1:00 to 4:00 / takes English classes

_____

5 after work / Li / to the library / takes the bus

_____

6 On Friday night / with my friends / go out / I

_____

7 with her boyfriend / Every Friday / eats out / she

_____

8 on weekends / Micah / with Jon / plays tennis

_____

Your turn ↶

Look at your second draft of Writing 1 and Writing 2. Can you put some time expressions at the beginning of your sentences? Remember to use a comma.

B Check for common mistakes

SUBJECT-VERB AGREEMENT

Many students make mistakes with subject-verb agreement. Look at these corrected mistakes.

      go
I ~~goes~~ to school at 7:45 a.m.

        don't
Marc and Denise ~~doesn't~~ drive to work.

      takes
He ~~take~~ the bus every morning.

        doesn't
Her brother ~~don't~~ exercise on weekdays.

Practice 11

Read about Imad and Hicham. Cross out the mistakes and write the corrections above them. There are seven more mistakes.

>   *take*
> ¹Imad and Hicham are brothers. ²They ~~takes~~ English language classes at Oxnard Community College. ³Hicham goes to school every day. ⁴Imad don't go to school every day. ⁵He take classes on Mondays and Wednesdays, and he works on the other days. ⁶Hicham don't have a job yet. ⁷He goes home after classes. ⁸He either does his homework or he work on his computer. ⁹He checks his e-mail and search the Internet for a job. ¹⁰Imad works in a restaurant. ¹¹In the evenings, Imad bring home food from the restaurant. ¹²Hicham and Imad doesn't cook dinner. ¹³They eat the food from Imad's restaurant.

C Edit your writing

Use the *Editing Checklist* below to edit your sentences. Look for only one kind of mistake each time you read your sentences. For example, the first time you read your sentences, ask yourself, "Does every sentence start with a capital letter?"

EDITING CHECKLIST ☑

☐ **1** Does every sentence start with a capital letter?

☐ **2** Does every sentence end with a period?

☐ **3** Do all your subjects and verbs agree?

☐ **4** Is there a variety of time expressions?

☐ **5** Are there commas after time expressions at the beginning of sentences?

D Write the final draft

Make all your changes on your second draft of Writing 1 and Writing 2. Remember to mark where the changes go. Rewrite each draft. Make any changes that you need.

A Share your writing

Follow these steps to share your writing.

1 Work with a partner. Read your partner's writing.
2 Discuss the similarities and differences in your weekday and weekend activities. For example, "We both sleep late on weekends."
3 Get into groups and share your similarities and differences.

B Check your progress

After you get your writing back from your teacher, complete the *Progress Check* below.

PROGRESS CHECK

Date: _____

New vocabulary I used: _____

_____

_____

New grammar I used: _____

_____

Connecting words I used: _____

Mechanics I learned: _____

Things I need to remember the next time I write: _____

_____

Families

Think about your family. Is it a big family or a small family? Do you have any sisters or brothers? Are you married or single? Who do you live with? Think about other families that you know well. What are they like? Are those families similar to your family?

In this chapter, you write about families.

A Useful vocabulary

Follow these steps to study words to use when you write about families.

1 Work with a partner. Talk about the words in the *Vocabulary Pool*. Together, check (✓) the words you both know, and highlight the ones you don't know.

VOCABULARY POOL

Nouns		Adjectives
aunt	half sister/brother	divorced
baby	husband	extended (family)
brother	in-laws	immediate (family)
brother-/sister-in-law	mother	older
child/children	mother-/father-in-law	pregnant
cousin	nephew	remarried
daughter	niece	younger
ex-wife/husband	only child	
father	parents	
generation	sister	
grandchild/son/daughter	son	
grandfather	stepmother/father/	
grandmother	sister/brother	
grandparents	twins	
great-grandchildren	uncle	
great-grandparents	wife	

2 Change partners. Look at your new partner's highlighted words. Explain them to your partner if you can.

3 With your new partner, look at this word map. Fill in the blanks with as many of the nouns from the *Vocabulary Pool* as you can. You may use some of them twice. When you finish, compare your word map with the rest of the class.

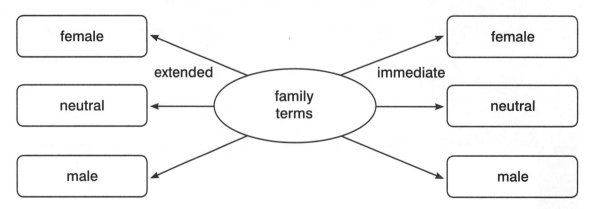

4 Tell your partner about your family. Use the words in the *Vocabulary Pool*.

B Vocabulary in context

Follow these steps to use and read words from the *Vocabulary Pool*.

- Work with a partner. Look at the family tree. Talk about the relationships between the people.
- Read about the family. Guess who is writing and write the name in the space next to the number below.
- Look back at the *Vocabulary Pool*. Look for words that are *not* in the family descriptions below. Find as many words as you can before your teacher tells you to stop.

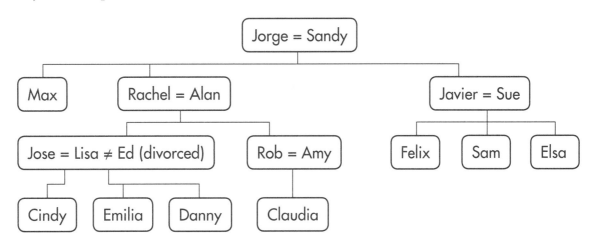

_____ 1   I have two brothers. We all still live with our parents. My father's sister lives with her parents, too. She and her husband have two children, but they don't live with my aunt and uncle. Both of my cousins have children. One of my cousins is divorced. His wife is remarried. She and her husband have a new baby.

_____ 2   We have a big, happy family. My wife and I have three children, a daughter and two sons. We also have five grandchildren. Our daughter has two children, and one of our sons has three children. One of our sons is single. He doesn't have children. Both of our daughter's children have children, so that means we are great-grandparents!

_____ 3   My wife and I live with her parents. They are very nice, and we get along well. Our two children are grown, but they live nearby. We see our three grandchildren a lot. Our younger son is divorced. He and his ex-wife have two children, and our older son and his wife have one child. My brother and sister-in-law have three children, so I have two nephews and one niece.

_____ 4   I have a brother and a stepsister. My brother is older, but he still plays with me. We get along pretty well. Our cousin lives nearby, and she plays with us sometimes, too. She's an only child, but not for long. Our aunt is pregnant! I'm happy because we need more cousins! Our extended family is growing.

C Get ideas

Follow these steps to get ideas to write about families.

1 On a separate piece of paper, draw your family tree. Include both your immediate and extended family. Write each person's name on the tree.

2 Work with a partner. Tell each other about your family trees. Use the words and phrases from the *Vocabulary Pool* to describe your tree.

3 Did your partner use any words that you can include in your family tree? Add them to your family tree.

D Freewrite

Freewrite about the topics below. For each topic, your teacher will tell you when to start and stop writing. Write everything that you think of, and don't worry about grammar or spelling. You can write words, phrases, and sentences. Don't stop to erase anything. Just keep writing.

Freewrite 1 Your immediate family

Freewrite 2 Your extended family

II PREPARING YOUR WRITING

A Learn about pronouns

SUBJECT AND OBJECT PRONOUNS

Pronouns replace nouns in sentences. Use a noun first, and then use a pronoun. This way, you don't have to repeat nouns.

Elsa has two cousins. **She** visits **them** every weekend.

Marc has a sister. **He** calls **her** once a week.

Jim and I live near our father. **We** have dinner with **him** every Wednesday.

Subject Pronouns	Object Pronouns
I	me
you	you
he	him
she	her
it	it
we	us
they	them

Practice 1

Read about Alicia and Fred. Then answer the questions.

> ¹Alicia and Fred are divorced. ²They have two children, Max and Sarah. ³Alicia lives in Fort Lauderdale. ⁴Max and Sarah live with her during the week. ⁵On the weekends, they live with Fred. ⁶Fred lives in Miami. ⁷Every Friday, he drives to Fort Lauderdale. ⁸He picks the children up and takes them to Miami for the weekend. ⁹Max and Sarah love Miami. ¹⁰Fred takes them to the zoo and museums. ¹¹Max and Sarah come back to Alicia on Sunday nights. ¹²They are always excited but tired then. ¹³Alicia helps them relax and get ready for the week.

1 Who is "they" in sentence 2? _____

2 Who is "her" in sentence 4? _____

3 Who is "they" in sentence 5? _____

4 Who is "he" in sentence 7? _____

5 Who is "them" in sentence 8? _____

6 Who is "them" in sentence 10? _____

Practice 2

Read about the Park family. Cross out each underlined noun. Write the correct subject or object pronoun above it.

> There are six people in the Park family. The Park family lives in South Korea.
> Samuel and Olivia Park are the parents. ~~Samuel and Olivia Park~~ *They* have
> (1)
> three children, Sarah, Richard, and Sophia. The two older children live with
> Samuel and Olivia Park. Sarah is 23 years old. Sarah works as a Web designer.
> (2)   (3)
> Richard is 22. Richard is also a Web designer. Richard works with Sarah, and
> (4)
> Sarah drives to work with Richard every day. Sophia is 18. Sophia is studying
> (5)   (6)
> English. Sophia is a student at Hampshire College. Hampshire College is in
> (7)
> Massachusetts. Hampshire College is two hours away from Boston.
> (8)
> Grandma Park lives with the Park family, too. Grandma Park is 72 years old.
> (9)
> Grandma Park cooks and takes art classes at the Senior Center. Grandma Park
> (10)   (11)
> likes the Senior Center because Grandma Park has many friends there.
> (12)   (13)

Practice 3

On a separate piece of paper, rewrite the sentences below. Use subject and object pronouns so that you don't repeat nouns.

American actress Rachel Liu is married to actor Barry Smith. Rachel and Barry live in Los Angeles. Rachel and Barry have four children. Brittany is 12 years old. Brittany is the oldest. Brad and Bart are 10 years old. Brad and Bart are twins. Beth is 8 years old. Beth is the baby of the family. During the week, Barry takes the children to school. Barry drives the children to three different schools each day. Rachel picks the children up and takes the children to classes in the afternoons. On the weekends, Rachel and Barry take the children to the baseball park. Rachel, Barry, Brittany, Brad, Bart, and Beth all love baseball!

B Learn about possessive nouns

POSSESSIVE NOUNS

To show possession, add 's or just an apostrophe (') to nouns.

- For all singular nouns, add 's.
  The boy**'s** father is a teacher.

- For all proper nouns that end in -s, add 's.
  Charles**'s** father is a teacher.

- For plural nouns that end in -s, add just the apostrophe (').
  The boys' father is a teacher.

- For irregular plural nouns that do not end in -s, add 's.
  The children**'s** father is a teacher.

Practice 4

Read about Claire's family. Add the missing apostrophes ('). There are six more mistakes.

¹Claire's immediate family is very big. ²That's because her parents are divorced. ³Claire has two brothers, one sister, and three stepbrothers. ⁴Claire lives at her mothers house during the week. ⁵She lives at her fathers house on the weekends. ⁶Her stepmother is very nice. ⁷Her name is Phyllis. ⁸Phylliss parents live nearby, so Claire knows them, too. ⁹All the children like to visit her parents. ¹⁰Claires family also includes a lot of pets. ¹¹For example, Phylliss parents have two cats, a bird, and a dog. ¹²The childrens favorite pet is Tweety, the bird.

POSSESSIVE PRONOUNS

Like possessive nouns, possessive pronouns also show possession. The possessive pronoun is always near the noun or subject pronoun that it replaces.

Elsa goes to school in Mexico City. **Her** university is famous.

My parents live in Oakland. **Their** house is huge.

Subject Pronouns	Possessive Pronouns
I	my
you	your
he	his
she	her
it	its
we	our
they	their

Practice 5

Fill in the blanks with the correct possessive pronoun.

1 You have a nice family. I know _____ parents well.

2 I have a big family because _____ brothers and sisters each have lots of children.

3 My in-laws love to play with _____ grandchildren. They are wonderful grandparents.

4 We have two boys and one girl. All of _____ children are still in school, so they still live at home.

5 I have two lovely nieces. _____ nieces both have children. That means I am a great-aunt!

6 Jon's cousins are very young, but _____ uncle is only two years older than Jon. They are good friends.

7 We gave _____ baby a long name. _____ name is Josafina Yolanda Magdalena Marielle.

8 Alexandra and _____ husband live with _____ husband's parents. _____ house is very large.

9 Frank and _____ wife have three children. _____ children live with them.

10 You and _____ mother are lucky because _____ homes are close together.

Practice 6

Complete the story with the correct possessive pronouns.

In some countries, a married man lives in _____ parents' home, so many
                                              (1)
women move into _____ in-laws' homes and live with _____
                     (2)   (3)
husbands' parents. In addition, after a husband and wife have children, the
woman raises _____ children in _____ in-laws' home. Often, the
                  (4)   (5)
woman takes care of both _____ children and _____ husband's
                              (6)   (7)
parents. For example, I am Turkish. _____ name is Nisran. I am married
                                         (8)
to Yasar, and I live in _____ in-laws' house with Yasar and _____
                             (9)   (10)
four children. I take care of _____ in-laws. I like to help them. But at
                                   (11)
night, I am often very tired. I fall into _____ bed early, and I fall asleep
                                              (12)
very quickly!

Practice 7

Look at the family tree in *Vocabulary in context* on page 57. Write sentences about
Jorge's family. Use possessive pronouns.

Examples: *Sandy is his wife. Max, Rachel, and Javier are their children.*

1 _____

2 _____

3 _____

4 _____

5 _____

6 _____

C Write the first draft

Now it's time to write the first draft of two pieces of writing. Use your freewrites and
your ideas and language from Sections I and II to help you. You can also add any
other ideas that come to mind.

Writing 1 Write a first draft about your immediate family.

Writing 2 Write a first draft about your extended family.

III REVISING YOUR WRITING

A Expand your vocabulary

> ### RELATIONSHIP PHRASES
>
> You can use these phrases to talk about your relationships with your family members.
>
> - *be close (to)*: be close to, be very close to, be not very close to
>   **I'm very close to** my younger sister, but **I'm not very close to** my cousins.
>
> - *get along (with)*: get along with, get along well with, not get along well with
>   **I get along well with** my parents, but **I don't get along well with** my sister.
>
> - *keep in touch (with)*: keep in touch with, don't keep in touch with
>   **I keep in touch with** my cousins, but **I don't keep in touch with** my uncle.
>
> - *have a good / bad relationship (with)*: have a good / bad relationship with, don't have a good relationship with
>   **I have a good relationship with** my mother, but **I have a bad relationship with** my father.

Practice 8

Fill in the blanks with the phrases below. More than one answer is possible in some sentences.

close	get along well	keep in touch	not have a good relationship
get along	have a good relationship	not get along	not very close

1 My brother never calls our cousins, but I _____ with them.

2 Josiah and his sister play together all the time. They are very _____.

3 Sometimes, Mei and Ying _____ with their parents well, but other times they do _____ with them at all.

4 Many parents say it is hard to _____ with their teenagers.

5 Twins are often _____ to each other.

6 Now that we are adults, my sister and I _____ with each other.

7 My grandparents have a computer, so I _____ with them by e-mail.

8 I fight with my ex-wife all the time. I do _____ with her at all.

Your turn

Look at your first draft of Writing 1 and Writing 2. On each draft, write sentences using relationship phrases. Remember to mark where these sentences go.

B Connect your ideas

> **USING AND AND BUT**
>
> You can use *and* and *but* to join two sentences. Use a comma before each connector.
>
> • Use *and* to connect similar ideas in a sentence.
>
> Jane and her cousin are the same age, **and** they go to the same school, too!
>
> • Use *but* to connect two contrasting ideas in a sentence.
>
> I get along with my older cousin, **but** I don't get along with my younger cousin.

Practice 9

Fill in the blanks with *and* or *but*.

1 My mother is an only child, _____ my father is an only child, too.

2 Most Japanese families are small, _____ Maki's family is big.

3 Sei Young and her cousin fight a lot, _____ they are very close.

4 Marco and Kristen both love sports, _____ they both play on teams.

5 Jack and Juliana are divorced, _____ they get along very well.

Practice 10

Read the story. Circle *and* or *but* to join the sentences. Then add five more missing commas.

Abigail's great-grandparents are old, and /(but) they seem very young. Abigail
(1)
and her cousins visit them often. Her great-grandmother likes to cook and / but
(2)
the children love to eat her treats. Sometimes the house is very noisy and crowded
and / but Abigail's great-grandparents don't mind. They like all the activity.
(3)
Sometimes the cousins play outside and / but the adults sit inside and talk. After
(4)
a while, Abigail's great-grandparents go upstairs to nap and / but sometimes
(5)
Abigail goes with them. Abigail is seven years old and / but she still likes to nap.
(6)

Your turn

Look at your first draft of Writing 1 and Writing 2. On each draft, write sentences about your immediate and extended families using *and* and *but*. Remember to mark where these sentences go.

C Give and get feedback

Work with a partner. Follow these steps to give and get feedback.

1 Show your partner your first draft of Writing 1 and Writing 2 with the sentences you added to them.

2 Exchange books. Answer the questions in the chart below about your partner's first drafts.

	Writing 1	Writing 2
How many words or phrases from the *Vocabulary Pool* did your partner use?		
How many subject and object pronouns did your partner use?		
How many possessive nouns did your partner use?		
How many possessive pronouns did your partner use?		
How many relationship phrases did your partner use?		
How many sentences have *and* or *but*?		

3 What do you like about each of your partner's pieces of writing? Underline two or three parts. Tell your partner.

4 Show your partner the chart. Discuss your answers. Do you have any suggestions for your partner?

5 Return your partner's book.

D Write the second draft

Follow these steps to write the second draft.

1 Look at the chart your partner completed for your first draft of Writing 1 and Writing 2. Think about what your partner said. Did your partner give you any ideas you can use? For example, can you use any more possessive pronouns?

2 Look at the *Progress Check* on page 54 of Chapter 3. Use it to help you revise your first draft of Writing 1 and Writing 2.

3 Rewrite each draft with the changes.

A Focus on mechanics

> ### USING CAPITAL LETTERS WITH NAMES AND FAMILY TERMS
>
> Use capital letters with people's names.
>
>   <u>A</u>ndy, <u>E</u>lsa, <u>F</u>red and <u>O</u>liver, <u>J</u>orge and <u>M</u>aria <u>R</u>uiz, the <u>S</u>miths
>
> Use capital letters with family terms when you use them like names.
>
>   <u>A</u>unt <u>C</u>laudia lives with me.
>
>   We are very close to <u>G</u>randma <u>R</u>ose.
>
> For more rules about capital letters, see Appendix B on page 162.

Practice 11

Read these sentences. Cross out eight more letters that should be capital letters and write the corrections above them. Then check your answers with a partner.

>   ¹I live with my daughter ^M~~m~~ary and her husband fred. ²Danielle is mary and fred's daughter (and my granddaughter). ³She lives here with us. ⁴We also live with my aunt. ⁵aunt linda is 80 years old, and we take care of her. ⁶fred's cousin lives with us, too. ⁷cousin jack is divorced, and he doesn't like living alone. ⁸We're a big, happy family!

Your turn

Check your use of capital letters in your second draft of Writing 1 and Writing 2.

B Check for common mistakes

> ### MISTAKES WITH MALE AND FEMALE PRONOUNS
>
> Many students confuse male and female pronouns. Look at these corrected mistakes.
>
>   *She*
>   Mary is my mother's cousin. ~~He~~ lives with us.
>
>   *her*
>   I visit Grandma Rose every weekend. I bring ~~him~~ flowers.

Practice 12

Read about Steve's family. Cross out seven more mistakes and write the corrections above them.

¹Divorce is difficult for many families, but not for some people. ²For example, Steve is divorced. ³~~She~~ *He* and her ex-wife, Brittany, have one child, Sophie. ⁴Steve's ex-wife is remarried. ⁵He and his new husband also have one child, Nick. ⁶Brittany and his husband live near Steve. ⁷Brittany and his husband get along very well with her. ⁸Sophie is a little older than Nick, but he and Nick get along very well, too.

C Edit your writing

Use the *Editing Checklist* below to edit your sentences. Look for only one kind of mistake each time you read your sentences. For example, the first time you read your sentences, ask yourself, "Does every sentence start with a capital letter?"

EDITING CHECKLIST ☑

☐ **1** Does every sentence start with a capital letter?

☐ **2** Does every sentence end with a period?

☐ **3** Did you use the correct subject, object, and possessive nouns and pronouns?

☐ **4** Is there a variety of family relationship phrases?

☐ **5** Do your sentences with *and* and *but* have two subjects, two verbs, and two objects?

☐ **6** Are there commas before *and* and *but* in sentences with two subjects, two verbs, and two objects?

☐ **7** Do you have correct capitalization for names and family terms?

D Write the final draft

Make all your changes on your second draft of Writing 1 and Writing 2. Remember to mark where the changes go. Rewrite each draft again. Make any changes that you need.

A Share your writing

Follow these steps to share your writing.

1 Work with a partner. Read each other's writing.
2 Ask and answer questions about your partner's family.
   For example, "Who is older, you or your brother?"
3 Present your partner's family to the class.
   For example, "Marta lives with her mother and her father. She has an older brother, but she doesn't get along with him."

B Check your progress

After you get your writing back from your teacher, complete the *Progress Check* below.

PROGRESS CHECK

Date: _____

New vocabulary I used: _____

_____

_____

New grammar I used: _____

_____

Connecting words I used: _____

Mechanics I learned: _____

Things I need to remember the next time I write: _____

_____

That's Entertainment!

Think about the types of entertainment that you enjoy. What TV shows do you usually watch? What are your favorite types of movies? How often do you go to the movies? Do you read books? What are your favorite types of books?

In this chapter, you write about TV, movies, or books.

A Useful vocabulary

Follow these steps to study words to use when you write about different types of entertainment.

1 Work with a partner. Talk about the words in the *Vocabulary Pool*. Together, check (✓) the words you both know, and highlight the ones you don't know.

VOCABULARY POOL

Types of Television Shows	Types of Movies	Types of Books
cartoon	action	biography
detective show	adventure	comic
documentary	animated	fantasy
drama	comedy	fiction
educational program	horror	history
game show	musical	how-to
news program	romance	mystery
reality show	science fiction	nonfiction
sitcom	thriller	science
soap opera	western	sci-fi
sports program		self-help

2 Change partners. Look at your new partner's highlighted words. Explain them to your partner if you can.

3 Read these TV show, movie, and book titles. What types are they? Discuss them with your partner. Then write two possible types for each TV show, movie, and book title.

Today's TV Schedule

1 The Mouse Math Detective

educational program

_____

2 Can You Become a Millionaire?

_____

_____

NEW MOVIES THIS WEEK

3 The Monster from Mars

_____

_____

4 My Husband, the Cowboy

_____

_____

New Books

5 How to Be a Better Parent

_____

_____

6 The Princess and the Robot

_____

_____

4 Choose a TV show, a movie, and a book title from step 3 that looks interesting to you. Tell your partner your choices. Why did you choose these titles?

B Vocabulary in context

Follow these steps to use and read words from the *Vocabulary Pool*.

- Work with a partner. Look at each picture. What type of TV show, movie, or book does it show? Discuss with your partner.
- Read about the types of entertainment the people below say they like and don't like.
- Write the letter(s) of the pictures that show the types of entertainment they like. Then write the letter(s) of the pictures that show what they don't like. Check your answers with a partner.

1   People in my country don't like to go to the movies. They usually watch TV in the cold winter months. They like American sitcoms, such as *Ray*, and Japanese game shows, such as *Komodo Dragon*. They don't enjoy dramas and other serious shows. People rarely watch those shows.

Like _____   Don't like _____

a

2   My brother likes to read books. He takes the bus to work every day and he reads on the bus. He doesn't enjoy fiction. He likes self-help books and books about famous people in history, such as biographies of kings. He likes to watch action movies sometimes, but he never watches TV.

Likes _____   Doesn't like _____

b

3   My parents go to the movies three or four times a month. They like a lot of different kinds of movies, such as comedies and action movies. They sometimes watch TV, but they only like the news.

Like _____   Don't like _____

c

4   My sister watches TV every night. She only likes educational programs, such as documentaries. She likes movies, too, but only very serious ones. She reads a lot. The books she reads are usually nonfiction, such as historical books.

Likes _____   Doesn't like _____

d

C Get ideas

Follow these steps to get ideas to write about entertainment.

1 Think about your favorite types of TV shows, movies, and books. Complete the chart below. Use the words from the *Vocabulary Pool*.

TV Shows	Movies	Books

2 Work with a partner. Compare charts. Tell your partner what types of TV shows, movies, and books you like. Tell you partner some titles of each.

3 Did your partner talk about any entertainment types that you like, too? Add them to your chart.

4 Stand up and walk around the room. Ask people about their favorite types of entertainment.

5 Find one person who shares two favorites from your chart. Sit down and discuss your favorites with that person.

D Freewrite

Freewrite about the topics below. For each topic, your teacher will tell you when to start and stop writing. Write everything that you think of, and don't worry about grammar or spelling. You can write words, phrases, and sentences. Don't stop to erase anything. Just keep writing.

Freewrite 1 Types of movies or books that you like and that you don't like

Freewrite 2 Popular types of TV shows in your country or culture

A Learn about adverbs of frequency

> ### ONE-WORD ADVERBS OF FREQUENCY
>
> *Adverbs of frequency* describe how often an action happens. We often use them with the simple present tense to talk about habits. Here are some common adverbs of frequency.
>
> None of the time   All of the time
>
> *never*   *rarely*   *sometimes*   *often*   *usually*   *always*
>
> We usually put these one-word adverbs of frequency after *be* and before other verbs.
>
> Hasan is **often** in front of his computer.
>
> My wife and I **sometimes** go to the movies.
>
> You can use *almost* in front of *never* and *always*, too.
>
> I **almost always** watch the news in the morning.

Practice 1

On a separate piece of paper, write these words in the right order to make sentences.

1 TV news shows / rarely / Aisha / watches

2 newspapers / read / never / My friends

3 We / get / from TV comedy shows / the news / often

4 on the Internet / usually / Sam / reads the news

5 almost never / Some people / TV / watch

6 are / about real events / usually / Movies / popular

Practice 2

Complete the following sentences about yourself. Use the adverbs of frequency in the box above. Talk about your sentences with a partner.

1 I _____ watch the news on TV.

2 I _____ read newspapers.

3 I _____ watch comedy shows on TV.

4 I _____ read the news on the Internet.

5 I _____ watch TV.

6 I _____ watch movies about real events.

B Learn more about adverbs of frequency

> **ADVERBS OF FREQUENCY PHRASES**
>
> Some adverbs of frequency are phrases. They usually go at the end of the sentence or at the beginning.
>
> Here are some common adverbs of frequency phrases.
>
> | | | | |
> |---|---|---|---|
> | once a day | twice a week | three times a month | four times a year |
> | every day | every week | every year | all the time |
>
> I brush my teeth **twice a day**.
>
> I go fishing **three times a year**.
>
> **Every year,** I go somewhere hot for my vacation.
>
> I work in my garden **every day**.

Practice 3

Read about Jamil's and Noor's habits. Then read the sentences below. Correct the adverbs of frequency to make the sentences true.

> Every day, Jamil gets up at 6:30 a.m. Then he turns on the TV and watches the news. He doesn't read the newspaper in the morning, except on Sundays. On most days, Jamil takes the train to work. On the train, he reads a book. Two or three times a week, he also works on the train. Jamil does not take the train to work every day. Four or five times a month, his friend, Rana, drives him to work instead. Jamil doesn't work or read in the car. Every day, Jamil takes the train home. In the evenings, he and his wife, Noor, almost never go out. They stay home and watch TV. They like to watch documentaries and educational TV programs together. Jamil also likes detective shows. He watches his favorite detective show once a week. Noor doesn't watch detective shows. She goes to bed instead.

1 Jamil watches the news on TV ~~twice a week~~. *every day*

2 Jamil reads the newspaper every day.

3 Jamil always takes the train to work.

4 Jamil rarely works on the train.

5 Rana often drives Jamil to work.

6 In the evenings, Jamil and Noor sometimes go to the movies.

7 Jamil and Noor watch educational shows and documentaries on TV on Sundays.

8 Jamil and Noor often watch detective shows together.

Practice 4

On a separate piece of paper, rewrite the story about Jamil and Noor. Change four or five of the sentences that have adverbs of frequency phrases. Rewrite those sentences with one-word adverbs of frequency. This will give the writing some variety.

Practice 5

Fill out the survey below. Then write sentences about yourself on a separate piece of paper. Use adverbs of frequency.

Complete the following form about your entertainment habits.

TV (hours a day): _____

How many nights a week do you watch these types of programs?

news programs: _____   educational programs: _____

reality shows: _____   sitcoms: _____

game shows: _____   sports programs: _____

Movies (times a month): _____

Rate the movie types from 1 to 5, with 5 being your favorite.

comedy: 1   2   3   4   5

romance: 1   2   3   4   5

action/adventure: 1   2   3   4   5

animated: 1   2   3   4   5

horror: 1   2   3   4   5

musical: 1   2   3   4   5

Books (hours a week): _____

How many of these types of books do you read a year?

fiction: _____   biography: _____   nonfiction: _____   sci-fi: _____   comic: _____

C Write the first draft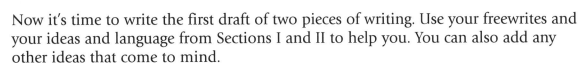

Now it's time to write the first draft of two pieces of writing. Use your freewrites and your ideas and language from Sections I and II to help you. You can also add any other ideas that come to mind.

Writing 1 Write a first draft about your favorite types of movies or books.

Writing 2 Write a first draft about popular types of TV shows in your country or culture.

A Expand your vocabulary

MAKING NOUNS INTO ADJECTIVES

You can use adjectives to add variety and interest to your sentences. You can make some nouns into adjectives when you add an adjective ending to a noun.

I like to watch shows with romance in them. → I like romantic shows.

Here are some common adjective endings.

-al   -ed   -ic   -ous

Practice 6

Work with a partner. Complete the charts below with the adjective forms. Use a dictionary, if necessary.

Noun	Adjective
animation	
biography	
drama	
education	

Noun	Adjective
information	
music	
mystery	
science	

Practice 7

Complete the sentences with adjectives from *Practice 6*. There is more than one correct answer. When you finish, compare your answers with a partner.

> Our favorite TV station is Channel 32. I like Channel 32's nightly news show. It's very _____ (1). I also often watch science programs, such as *Science Today*. The _____ (2) topics are always interesting. The children's _____ (3) programs are great. My children often watch *Counting Is Fun*. My husband is very _____ (4). He likes *Night at the Opera*. I like it, too. Opera stories usually are very _____ (5). In the stories, people often fall in love and then die.

Your turn ∿

Look at your first draft of Writing 1 and Writing 2. On each draft, rewrite some sentences with the adjective forms of the nouns. Remember to mark where these sentences go.

B Connect your ideas

USING SUCH AS

You can use *such as* to introduce examples. Use *such as* immediately before the example.

I like science fiction movies, **such as** *Star Trek*.

Marta often reads historical novels, **such as** *Gone with the Wind* and *The Six Wives of Henry VIII*.

Reality shows, **such as** *So You Want to Be a Celebrity*, are very popular in the United States.

Note: We usually use a comma before examples that are introduced by *such as*.

Practice 8

Rewrite the sentences with *such as*. Use the TV shows, movies, and books below as examples.

Escape from Bald Mountain	*My Life*	*SuperStar*
I Want to Be a Millionaire	*Nightmare Street*	*The Middle Ages*
Monsters Under the Sea	*Storm Chasers*	*The Nightly News*

1 I often watch reality shows.

_____

2 Many older people like to watch news programs.

_____

3 Horror movies are often on TV late at night.

_____

4 Biographies are very popular.

_____

5 My son likes to read children's adventure stories.

_____

6 He usually reads history books for school.

_____

Your turn ↷

Look at your first draft of Writing 1 and Writing 2. On each draft, write or rewrite some sentences with *such as*. Remember to mark where these sentences go.

C Give and get feedback

Work with a partner. Follow these steps to give and get feedback.

1 Show your partner your first draft of Writing 1 and Writing 2 with the sentences you added to them.

2 Exchange books. Answer the questions in the chart below about your partner's pieces of writing.

	Writing 1	Writing 2
How many words from the *Vocabulary Pool* did your partner use?		
How many one-word adverbs of frequency did your partner use?		
How many adverbs of frequency phrases did your partner use?		
How many adjective forms of nouns did your partner use?		
How many sentences use *such as*?		

3 What do you like about each of your partner's pieces of writing? Underline two or three parts. Tell your partner.

4 Show your partner the chart. Discuss your answers. Do you have any suggestions for your partner?

5 Return your partner's book.

D Write the second draft

Follow these steps to write the second draft.

1 Look at the chart your partner completed for your first draft of Writing 1 and Writing 2. Think about what your partner said. Did your partner give you any ideas that you can use? For example, can you add any more sentences with *such as*?

2 Look at the *Progress Check* on page 68 of Chapter 4. Use it to help you revise your first draft of Writing 1 and Writing 2.

3 Rewrite each draft with the changes.

IV EDITING YOUR WRITING

A Focus on mechanics

USING UNDERLINING AND ITALICS

<u>Underline</u> the titles of TV shows, movies, and books when you write by hand.

We both enjoy detective shows, such as <u>Law and Order</u> and <u>CSI</u>.

I like going to romantic comedies, such as <u>The Break-Up</u>.

My favorite book is <u>The Notebook</u>.

When you type on a computer, put titles of TV shows, movies, and books in *italics*. Follow these steps to use italics in Microsoft Word.

1 Use the mouse to highlight the title.

2 Click the *I* (italics) button on the toolbar.

To take the italics off, click the *I* button a second time.

Practice 9

Read and <u>underline</u> 11 more book and movie titles.

¹I am in a book club. ²We meet every six weeks to discuss books. ³We enjoy reading historical novels by women, such as <u>Wuthering Heights</u>, Wide Sargasso Sea, and The Other Boleyn Girl. ⁴Sometimes we read novels by men, too. ⁵We read books by Cormac McCarthy, such as The Road, and books by Pat Conroy, such as The Water Is Wide. ⁶We also like reading sci-fi books, such as Dune and Brave New World. ⁷We often read fantasy novels, too. ⁸We like The Lord of the Rings and other books by J. R. R. Tolkien. ⁹We also like J. K. Rowling's books, especially the first one, Harry Potter and the Philosopher's Stone. ¹⁰We rarely read nonfiction. ¹¹Sometimes we watch movies together, too. ¹²We watch movies of the books we read, such as My Sister's Keeper, The Time Traveler's Wife, and Inkheart.

Your turn

Check your use of underlining or italics in your second draft of Writing 1 and Writing 2.

B Check for common mistakes

PLACEMENT OF ADVERBS

Many students make mistakes with the placement of adverbs.

One-word adverbs of frequency usually go before the verb or after *be*.

He reads (often) news magazines.

(Always) animal documentaries are interesting to me.

Adverbs of frequency phrases can go at the beginning or at the end of the sentence. Use a comma when they go at the beginning.

She watches (once a year) a musical.

He (twice a week) reads the newspaper.

Practice 10

Read the text below. Circle the adverbs of frequency that are in an incorrect place, and draw an arrow to their correct place. Add commas, if necessary. Find seven more mistakes.

¹My family does different things in the evenings. ²My parents go (often) to the movies on weekends. ³They usually are excited about sci-fi movies, such as *Star Trek* and *The Matrix*. ⁴Almost never my grandparents go to the movies. ⁵They usually stay home and watch TV. ⁶My sister and I rarely stay home on weekends. ⁷We love the movies, but we don't like the same kind of movies. ⁸I like musicals, such as *Hairspray* and *Mamma Mia*. ⁹My sister goes to musicals never. ¹⁰She every week goes to scary horror movies, such as *Friday the 13th*. ¹¹My little brother goes almost never out in the evenings. ¹²He watches cartoons always on TV. ¹³He also watches reality shows, such as *The Amazing Race*, often.

C Edit your writing

Use the *Editing Checklist* below to edit your sentences. Look for only one kind of mistake each time you read your sentences. For example, the first time you read your sentences, ask yourself, "Does every sentence start with a capital letter?"

EDITING CHECKLIST ✓

- ☐ 1 Does every sentence start with a capital letter?
- ☐ 2 Does every sentence end with a period?
- ☐ 3 Are your adverbs of frequency in the right place?
- ☐ 4 Do you have the correct ending for adjective forms?
- ☐ 5 Did you use underlining or italics for titles?

D Write the final draft

Make all your changes on your second draft of Writing 1 and Writing 2. Remember to mark where the changes go. Rewrite each draft. Make any changes that you need.

V FOLLOWING UP

A Share your writing

Follow these steps to share your writing.

1 Work with a partner. Read your partner's writing.
2 Discuss the similarities and differences in your entertainment choices. For example, "We both like game shows on TV. We usually watch game shows on weekday nights." "You don't usually read books, but I sometimes read books."
3 Get into groups and share your similarities and differences.

B Check your progress

After you get your writing back from your teacher, complete the *Progress Check* below.

PROGRESS CHECK

Date: _____

New vocabulary I used: _____

_____

_____

New grammar I used: _____

_____

Connecting words I used: _____

Mechanics I learned: _____

Things I need to remember the next time I write: _____

_____

People

Think about the people you know. What do they look like? What are their personalities like? Think about a famous person. What does that person look like? What does that person seem like?

In this chapter, you write about people.

A Useful vocabulary

Follow these steps to study words to use when you write about people.

1 Work with a partner. Talk about the words in the *Vocabulary Pool*. Together, check (✓) the words you both know, and highlight the ones you don't know.

VOCABULARY POOL

athletic	cute	intelligent	short
average looking	dark	kind	shy
average-sized	elderly	light	sociable
bald	energetic	long	straight
beautiful	fashionable	medium height	strong
blond	friendly	messy	talented
brave	funny	middle-aged	tall
calm	generous	neat	thin
casual	good-looking	outgoing	thoughtful
confident	handsome	patient	young
considerate	happy	pretty	
cooperative	helpful	quiet	
curly	independent	serious	

2 Change partners. Look at your new partner's highlighted words. Explain them to your partner if you can.

3 With your partner, complete the chart with words from the *Vocabulary Pool*. Some words can go in more than one column.

Words that Describe Appearance	Words that Describe Hair	Words that Describe Personality
cute	blond	brave

4 Think of a friend. Then tell your partner about that friend. Use the words in the chart above.

B Vocabulary in context

Follow these steps to use and read words from the *Vocabulary Pool*.

- Work with a partner. Look at the picture and describe each person.
- Read the descriptions below. Match each description to a person in the picture. In the box next to the description, write the letter of the person described. Two people in the picture are not described.
- Explain your choices to your partner.

1   Mike is my neighbor. He's also a good friend. Mike is very tall and good-looking. He has short dark hair. He's strong and extremely athletic. Mike plays a lot of sports. He plays tennis, soccer, football, and basketball, of course. We often play tennis or basketball together.

2   Jake isn't tall, but he isn't short. He's average-sized. He has very curly dark hair. Jake is energetic. Jake is very smart, too. He gets good grades, and he always tells interesting stories. Jake's extremely considerate. He likes to be helpful.

3   My friends Toby and Alicia are married. They are both very tall and good-looking. Toby has long dark hair, and Alicia has short blond hair. They are also very outgoing. They seem really happy together.

4   Hannah has fairly long brown hair and light eyes. She's very cute. Hannah is a lovely person, but she is quiet and a bit shy. She doesn't talk very much, but she's a good listener. She helps me with my problems. She always has good advice.

5   Mason is Hannah's brother. He is very handsome. His hair is short, and he has big light eyes. He's fairly tall. Mason is an extremely outgoing, confident person. He's very independent, but he's also cooperative. He's fun to work with.

C Get ideas

Follow these steps to get ideas to write about people.

1 Draw the faces of three friends. Then draw the face of the famous person you wrote about in Chapter 3. Write the names of each person and four description words from the *Vocabulary Pool* below each name.

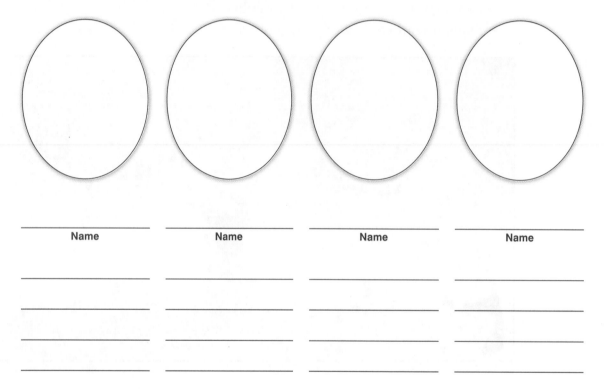

Name	Name	Name	Name
_____	_____	_____	_____
_____	_____	_____	_____
_____	_____	_____	_____
_____	_____	_____	_____

2 Work with a partner. Tell each other about the people in your drawings. For example, "This is my friend, Ka-eun. She's tall and thin. She's very pretty. She's very generous, too. She helps people a lot."

3 Did your partner use any description words that you can use for your friends? Add those words above.

D Freewrite

Freewrite about the topics below. For each topic, your teacher will tell you when to start and stop writing. Write everything that you think of, and don't worry about grammar or spelling. You can write words, phrases, and sentences. Don't stop to erase anything. Just keep writing.

Freewrite 1 Your friends

Freewrite 2 A famous person

A Learn about adjectives

ADJECTIVES

Adjectives describe nouns. They have the same form when they describe both singular and plural nouns. Don't add an *-s* ending to an adjective that describes a plural noun.

Adjectives help the reader see, hear, and feel the nouns you write about. They make your writing more interesting.

Put adjectives before the nouns they describe.

Mario has **dark** hair.

He is a **tall** man.

You also put adjectives after verbs such as *be, seem,* and *look.*

They are **energetic**.

Lydia seems **confident**.

Meghan and Paolo look **athletic**.

When there are two adjectives, we often put the adjective that describes size first.

She has **big beautiful** eyes.

Practice 1

Read this description of a movie star. Circle the adjectives, then draw arrows to the nouns or pronouns they describe.

¹George Clooney is very (famous). ²He acts in different types of movies. ³In some movies, he's serious. ⁴In other movies, he's funny. ⁵He is very talented. ⁶He's also very handsome. ⁷He has big brown eyes and short gray hair. ⁸He is average-sized. ⁹He's not tall, but he's not short. ¹⁰He is middle-aged, but he looks young. ¹¹In interviews, he seems intelligent. ¹²He tells interesting stories and funny jokes. ¹³He's not shy at all. ¹⁴He seems very outgoing. ¹⁵He seems very thoughtful and very nice.

Practice 2

Read about Zadie and Robert. Then answer the questions. Write complete sentences.

> Zadie and Robert are married. Zadie is average-sized. She is very pretty. She has short dark hair and light brown skin. She has big brown eyes. She is outgoing and friendly. She usually looks very happy. She also seems funny and smart. Robert is very tall and thin. He is average looking. He has blond hair and blue eyes. Robert is fairly quiet and shy, and he's extremely considerate of others. He seems very intelligent. Zadie and Robert are different, but they have a very happy marriage.

1 What does Zadie's hair look like?

_____

2 What color are Zadie's eyes?

_____

3 What color is Robert's hair?

_____

4 How handsome is Robert?

_____

5 What is Zadie's personality like?

_____

6 What is Robert's personality like?

_____

7 What kind of marriage do Zadie and Robert have?

_____

Practice 3

Look at the two driver's licenses. On a separate piece of paper, write sentences to describe the drivers. Use *be*, *seem*, and *look*.

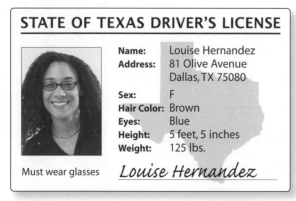

STATE OF TEXAS DRIVER'S LICENSE

Name:	Louise Hernandez
Address:	81 Olive Avenue Dallas, TX 75080
Sex:	F
Hair Color:	Brown
Eyes:	Blue
Height:	5 feet, 5 inches
Weight:	125 lbs.

Must wear glasses   *Louise Hernandez*

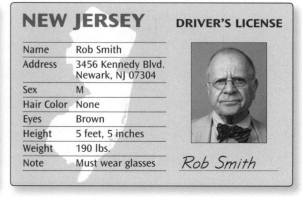

NEW JERSEY DRIVER'S LICENSE

Name	Rob Smith
Address	3456 Kennedy Blvd. Newark, NJ 07304
Sex	M
Hair Color	None
Eyes	Brown
Height	5 feet, 5 inches
Weight	190 lbs.
Note	Must wear glasses

Rob Smith

B Learn more about adjectives

INTENSIFIERS

Intensifiers add meaning to adjectives. Intensifiers make adjectives weaker or stronger.

Weakest			Strongest
not very	*fairly*	*very*	*extremely*

Intensifiers always come before the adjective.

She seems **fairly** shy.

Robert is **very** tall.

Mariel is an **extremely** generous person.

Practice 4

Put these words in the right order to make sentences.

1 Marco / athletic player / extremely / is / an
Marco is an extremely athletic player.

2 The students / casual / fairly / clothes / wear

3 The twins / have / outgoing / mother / very / a

4 Claudia / quiet / fairly / seems

5 Wei / very / guy / nice / is / a

6 Our teacher / extremely / helpful / is

7 My brother / thin / isn't / very

8 Inga / fairly / is / sociable

9 Yuta / very / hair / doesn't have / long

Practice 5

Look at the chart below. On a separate piece of paper, write sentences that describe each person. Use intensifiers. Compare your sentences with a partner. With your partner, choose one person to write about. Together, write five sentences below the chart.

	Jim	Eric	Sam
Age in years	22	51	83
Height in feet / cm	7'4" / 224 cm	5'3" / 160 cm	5'10" / 178 cm
IQ	100	150	120
Interesting fact	Has an Olympic gold medal for basketball	Third-place winner, Oak Street Cooking Contest	Volunteers at the hospital and helps in the schools

1 _____

2 _____

3 _____

4 _____

5 _____

C Write the first draft

Now it's time to write the first draft of two pieces of writing. Use your freewrites and your ideas and language from Sections I and II to help you. You can also add any other ideas that come to mind.

Writing 1 Choose one friend and write about him or her.

Writing 2 Write about a famous person.

A Expand your vocabulary

> **SYNONYMS**
>
> Synonyms are words that have almost the same meaning, for example, *little* and *small*. Use synonyms in your writing instead of repeating the same word.
>
> René is good-looking. His friend Gabe is also ~~good-looking~~. *(attractive)*
>
> You can find synonyms for many words in a *thesaurus*. A thesaurus is a collection of synonyms. Look for a thesaurus online or in the reference section of a library. If you are using Microsoft Word, you can also find a thesaurus in Tools.
>
> Be careful to check synonyms in a dictionary before you use them. A dictionary can show you if a word has two different meanings. For example, two synonyms for *funny* are *amusing* and *strange*. However, *amusing* and *strange* mean different things.
>
> John often tells **funny** jokes. (**amusing**)
>
> The weather is **funny** today. (**strange**)
>
> If you check the meaning of *funny* in a dictionary, you will not make the following mistakes.
>
> John often tells strange jokes.
>
> The weather is amusing today.

Practice 6

Look up the following adjectives in a thesaurus. List one or two synonyms for each one.

Adjective	Synonyms
1 pretty	
2 nice	
3 intelligent	
4 interesting	
5 happy	

Practice 7

Read about Flavia. Underline the adjectives. Use the chart in *Practice 6* to find a synonym for adjectives used more than once. Write the synonym above the adjective.

> ¹Flavia is a very pretty young woman in my class. ²She has pretty eyes.
> *attractive*
> ³She also has nice hair. ⁴She has a nice smile. ⁵She's intelligent, too. ⁶In our
> discussions, she always says very intelligent things. ⁷She's an interesting person,
> too. ⁸She tells interesting stories about her life. ⁹She also has interesting
> hobbies. ¹⁰She travels a lot, and she takes pretty pictures. ¹¹Flavia always seems
> happy, too. ¹²She has a lot of friends because happy people are fun to be with.

Your turn

Look at your first draft of Writing 1 and Writing 2. On each draft, rewrite some sentences using synonyms for any adjectives that you use more than once. Remember to mark where these sentences go.

B Connect your ideas

USING FOR EXAMPLE

You can use *for example* at the beginning of sentences to give more information.

  Marcia is outgoing and helpful. **For example,** she always helps new students.

  Wei is very generous. **For example,** he often shares things with his friends.

Use a comma after *for example*.

Practice 8

Match the sentences with their example sentences. Check your answers with a partner.

__f__ 1 Chris is fashionable.

_____ 2 My friend is an extremely calm person.

_____ 3 Margo's cousin is really considerate.

_____ 4 Lee isn't very athletic.

_____ 5 My classmate isn't a very happy person.

_____ 6 Robin is a very strong person.

a For example, she complains about everything a lot.

b For example, she never cries during movies.

c For example, he doesn't exercise very often.

d For example, he always asks about his friends' problems.

e For example, she never gets nervous before exams.

f For example, he only wears expensive jeans.

Practice 9

Work with a partner. Read the sentences. Think of example sentences to add.

1 My neighbors are very sociable.
   For example, they have big dinner parties a lot.

2 Sandy is a little quiet.

3 There are a lot of elderly people in my neighborhood.

4 My brother's children are very talented.

5 The teachers in that school are extremely patient.

6 My little boy isn't very independent.

7 Sondra's uncle isn't very generous.

8 Jorge is extremely nice.

9 Ally isn't very strong.

10 Gabriel is extremely messy.

Your turn

Look at your first draft of Writing 1 and Writing 2. On each draft, add sentences with *for example*. Remember to mark where these sentences go. For your draft of Writing 2, find some information about the famous person on the Internet to help you with example sentences.

C Give and get feedback

Work with a partner. Follow these steps to give and get feedback.

1 Show your partner your first draft of Writing 1 and Writing 2 with the sentences you added to them.

2 Exchange books. Answer the questions in the chart below about your partner's drafts.

	Writing 1	Writing 2
How many words from the *Vocabulary Pool* did your partner use?		
How many adjectives did your partner use?		
How many intensifiers did your partner use?		
How many synonyms did your partner use?		
How many sentences are there with *for example*?		

3 What do you like about each of your partner's pieces of writing? Underline two or three parts. Tell your partner.

4 Show your partner the chart. Discuss your answers. Do you have any suggestions for your partner?

5 Return your partner's book.

D Write the second draft

Follow these steps to write the second draft.

1 Look at the chart your partner completed for your first draft of Writing 1 and Writing 2. Think about what your partner said. Did your partner give you any ideas you can use? For example, can you use any sentences with *for example*?

2 Look at the *Progress Check* on page 82 of Chapter 5. Use it to help you revise your draft of Writing 1 and Writing 2.

3 Rewrite each draft with the changes.

A Focus on mechanics

CHECKING SPELLING

How do you know if you spelled your words correctly or not? Are you writing on paper or on a computer?

On paper

Follow these steps to correct misspelled words on paper.

- Look at the spelling of your words. Are there any words that you are not sure about?
- Underline these words.
- Then look them up in a dictionary.
- Write the correct spelling of these words in a personal spelling list. Keep this list with you when you write. You can use it to check words.

On a computer

On a computer, words with a red line under them may not have the correct spelling. Follow these steps to correct misspelled words on a computer.

- Select the word with the red line.
- Click on **Tools**. Then select **Spelling and Grammar**.
- Look at the list of **Suggestions**. Do you know these words? If you are not sure if you have the right word, check it in the dictionary.
- Select the word you want. Then click **Change**.

Practice 10

Read about this movie star. Find five words that are not spelled correctly. Cross them out and write the corrections above the words.

> ¹Joseph Gordon-Levitt is a talented young actor. ²He's not very tall, but he's very good-looking. ³He has short dark hair and beatiful eyes. ⁴In some movies, he is very funny, but in some movies, he's very serious. ⁵For example, in the movie *500 Days of Summer*, he's funny and serious. ⁶In the magazines, his clothes are casual but extremily fashionable. ⁷He also seems intresting and inteligent. ⁸He tells jokes a lot, and seems like an outgoing, frendly person.

Practice 11

Type the underlined words on a computer. Select them and go to **Spelling and Grammar**. Write the **Suggestions** on the line. Then find the **Suggestions** in a dictionary and circle the correct word.

1 The president of the company is an extremely <u>bussy</u> person. He works 14 hours a day.
(busy,) bossy, buss, bushy

2 My great-grandmother is still very <u>healty</u>. She is almost never sick.

3 Terry is a very <u>famousse</u> basketball coach.

4 Mike is a very <u>possitive</u> person. For example, he always smiles.

5 Judy's hair is blond and really <u>curley</u>.

6 My best friend usually wears casual clothes. She likes to feel <u>confortable</u>.

7 Leah is usually calm, but she feels <u>nervious</u> about the exam.

8 Cristina's family in the Philippines is very <u>weathy</u>.

Your turn ↲

Check your spelling in your second draft of Writing 1 and Writing 2.

B Check for common mistakes

USING WRITING WORDS, NOT SPEAKING WORDS

Some words and phrases are acceptable in speaking, but not in writing. In the column on the left are some intensifiers that we use mainly in speaking. Try to avoid these in writing. Use the synonyms in the column on the right instead.

Speaking	Writing
My best friend is **pretty** tall.	My best friend is **fairly** tall.
My best friend is **so** kind.	My best friend is **very** kind.
My teacher is **totally** smart.	My teacher is **extremely** smart.

Practice 12

Find four more speaking words in the following description. Cross them out and write correct writing words above them.

¹My boyfriend, Chang-hee, is a great person. ²He's s̶o̶ ^{very} smart. ³He speaks three languages, and he gets good grades in every class. ⁴He's totally good-looking, too. ⁵He has dark hair, and he's pretty tall. ⁶Chang-hee is so nice to everybody. ⁷He's very friendly, and he's also so helpful. ⁸All of my friends like him.

C Edit your writing

Use the *Editing Checklist* below to edit your sentences. Look for only one kind of mistake each time you read your sentences. For example, the first time you read your sentences, ask yourself, "Does every sentence start with a capital letter?"

EDITING CHECKLIST ✓

- ☐ **1** Does every sentence start with a capital letter?
- ☐ **2** Does every sentence end with a period?
- ☐ **3** Are the adjectives in the right place?
- ☐ **4** Did you use synonyms instead of repeating adjectives?
- ☐ **5** Did you use writing words instead of speaking words?
- ☐ **6** Did you spell all your words correctly?

D Write the final draft

Make all your changes on your second draft of Writing 1 and Writing 2. Remember to mark where the changes go. Rewrite each draft. Make any changes that you need. This time, type your drafts on a computer.

A Share your writing

Follow these steps to share your writing.

1 Get into groups of 3 or 4 students. Pass Writing 1 to the classmate on your right.

2 Read Writing 1 from your classmate. Does it seem like anyone you know? Complete the chart below.

3 Now pass your classmate's Writing 1 to the person on your right. Then read the new Writing 1.

4 Again, think of a person you know who is similar. Add that person to the chart.

5 Repeat three times or until you have your paper back.

6 Tell your classmates about the names you wrote down. Explain how they are similar to the people in the papers you read. For example, "Franco's paper is about his friend Georgio. Georgio sounds like my friend Sam. Sam is also outgoing and energetic."

Student Author	Person Described	This person seems like
Franco	*Franco's friend Georgio*	*my friend Sam*

B Check your progress

After you get your writing back from your teacher, complete the *Progress Check* below.

PROGRESS CHECK
Date: _____
New vocabulary I used: _____
_____
_____
New grammar I used: _____
_____
Connecting words I used: _____
Mechanics I learned: _____
Things I need to remember the next time I write: _____
_____

Jobs and Careers

Think about people with interesting jobs or careers. What do they do? Where do they work? Who do they work with? Now think about yourself. What about you? What kind of job or career do you have or want to have?

In this chapter, you write about jobs and careers.

A Useful vocabulary

Follow these steps to study words and phrases to use when you write about jobs and careers.

1 Work with a partner. Talk about the words and phrases in the *Vocabulary Pool*. Together, check (✓) the words you both know, and highlight the ones you don't know.

VOCABULARY POOL

Jobs	Actions	Work With	
accountant	assist	adults	medication
administrative assistant	be responsible for	advice	menus
architect	build	animals	money
chef	cook	buildings	patients
computer technician	create	children	people
contractor	cure	clothes	plants
cook	design	computers	safety
doctor	develop	diseases	students
fashion designer	diagnose	equipment	technology
gardener	fix	food	tests
home health aide	give	gardens	tools
lab technician	manage	houses	Web sites
landscaper	prepare	information	workers
nurse	repair	ingredients	
teacher	take care of		
veterinarian	teach		
Web designer	treat		

2 Change partners. Look at your new partner's highlighted words. Explain them to your partner if you can.

3 With your partner, complete the chart with words from the *Vocabulary Pool*. Match five jobs with words from the "Actions" and "Work With" columns.

A(n) . . .	does this . . .	with . . .
nurse	*takes care of*	*patients*

B Vocabulary in context

Follow these steps to use and read words and phrases from the *Vocabulary Pool*.

- Work with a partner. Look at the pictures. Talk about the job each person has.
- Read the descriptions below. Match each description to a picture. Write the letter in the blank. There are two extra pictures. Choose a job title from the *Vocabulary Pool* to complete the description.

_____ **1** These people assist doctors. They record basic information about patients. They give shots and medications. They also give patients and their families advice. I want to be a(n) _____ because I like to help people.

_____ **2** These people design and create gardens. They take care of flowers, plants, trees, and lawns. I like to work outdoors and use my hands, so I want to be a(n) _____.

_____ **3** These people take care of animals. They work indoors and outdoors. They work with their hands. They work alone and sometimes on teams. They often have assistants. They give advice to people about their animals. I like animals, so I want to be a(n) _____.

_____ **4** These people develop menus. They order ingredients and prepare food. They manage workers. They are also responsible for food safety. I want to be a(n) _____ because I like to work indoors. I also like to work on a team.

C Get ideas

Follow these steps to get ideas to write about jobs and careers.

1 Answer the questions on the careers quiz.

CAREER QUIZ!

Take this quiz to help you think about the perfect career for you. Circle the words that are true for you. You can circle more than one.

1. I like to work: outside / inside
2. I like to work with: children / adults / plants / food / numbers / computers / information
3. At work, I want to use my: hands / mind
4. I want to work: part-time / full-time
5. I like to work: alone / on a team
6. At work, I like to: fix things / make things / take care of things / study things / make things look nice
7. At work, I like to: help people / give advice to people / take care of people / solve problems / try new things
8. My favorite subject in school is: art / science / music / math / languages / literature / technology
9. I prefer to: follow instructions / give instructions
10. I like / don't like to meet new people.
11. I like / don't like to organize things.
12. I like to work: in the mornings / in the afternoons / in the evenings
13. I want to work in a: school / lab / factory / store / restaurant / hotel / office / garden / hospital

2 Get into small groups. Tell each other about the words you circled. Give reasons for circling these words. Try to use words from the *Vocabulary Pool* in your discussion.

3 Talk with your group. Match jobs from the *Vocabulary Pool* with some of the words you circled. What job matches your answers? For example, "Gardeners work outside. Home health aides solve problems."

D Freewrite

Freewrite about the topics below. For each topic, your teacher will tell you when to start and stop writing. Write everything that you think of, and don't worry about grammar or spelling. You can write words, phrases, and sentences. Don't stop to erase anything. Just keep writing.

Freewrite 1 Jobs you want to have in the future

Freewrite 2 A job you have or someone you know has now

A Learn about count and non-count nouns

COUNT AND NON-COUNT NOUNS

Nouns can be things you can count. *Count nouns* can be singular and plural.

                 singular   plural
The doctor treated one <u>patient</u> yesterday and five <u>patients</u> today.

Make singular count nouns into plural count nouns with an *-s*, *-es*, or *-ies*.

- Add *-s* to nouns ending in most consonants
- Add *-es* to nouns ending in *-ch*, *-x*, or *-s*
- Add *-ies* to nouns ending in *-y*

For more rules about adding *-s* or *-es*, see Appendix C on page 163.

Note these irregular plurals.

    man ➜ men   woman ➜ women
    child ➜ children   person ➜ people

Nouns can also be things you can't count. *Non-count nouns* never take plural endings.

    The doctor gives lots of good ~~advices~~.

Here are some examples of count nouns and non-count nouns.

Count Nouns	Non-count Nouns
one job	work
two bosses	time
three babies	health

For more common non-count nouns, see Appendix E on page 165.

Practice **1**

Read the list of nouns. Write *C* next to each count noun. Write *NC* next to each non-count noun. Then write the plural form of each count noun. You can use a dictionary.

1 hotel   *C hotels*   8 information   _____

2 technology _____   9 money   _____

3 disease _____   10 technician _____

4 chef _____   11 advice _____

5 art _____   12 cashier _____

6 healthcare _____   13 aide _____

7 nurse _____   14 education _____

Practice 2

Read this job description and circle the correct nouns. Then look at the nouns you circled. Write *S* above the singular count nouns. Write *P* above the plural count nouns. Highlight the non-count nouns. You can use a dictionary to help you.

A landscaper / (Landscapers) design gardens. A landscaper is like
      (1)   *P*

an artist / artists. First, a landscaper needs to visit people's homes to see their
      (2)

gardens. Then they choose the colors and the types of plant / plants for the
          (3)

garden. They look at the sunshine / sunshines in the garden. Then they have to
      (4)

make a plan for the garden. Landscapers do many different thing / things. They
      (5)

take care of the plants. I like art / arts, and I like plant / plants, so I want to
      (6)   (7)

be a landscaper or a gardener. I also like to do creative work / works. Designing
      (8)

gardens is very creative. It takes a lot of time / times, but it is very interesting.
      (9)

B Learn more about count and non-count nouns

ARTICLES A / AN, THE, OR Ø (NO ARTICLE)

The articles *a* and *an* are used only with singular count nouns. Use them when you don't need to be specific.

> I need to talk to **a** doctor.   (any doctor)
>
> **An** electrician fixes electrical problems.   (all electricians)

The article *the* is used with singular count nouns, plural count nouns, and non-count nouns. Use *the* when you need to be specific.

> I need to talk to **the** doctor in room 203.   (a specific doctor, the doctor in room 203)
>
> Eli manages **the** workers in Building A.   (specific workers, the workers in Building A)
>
> Marco makes **the** food at our restaurant.   (specific food, the food at our restaurant)

Use no article (Ø) to talk about count and non-count nouns in a very general way.

> Doctors work with patients.
>
> Technology is interesting.

Practice 3

Complete the sentences below with *A, a, An, an, The, the,* or Ø. In some sentences, there are two possible answers.

1   __Ø__ nurses have _____ important job. They assist _____ doctors. _____
    (1)   (2)   (3)   (4)

nurse at my doctor's office is very helpful. She gives _____ advice and tells _____
                                                        (5)   (6)

patients about useful Web sites.

2   My brother is _____ administrative assistant at _____ hospital. _____
                  (1)   (2)   (3)

administrative assistants at _____ hospital are unhappy because _____ hospital is
                             (4)   (5)

noisy and _____ doctors are not polite.
          (6)

3   I want to be _____ Green Gardener. I need to get _____ information about
                 (1)   (2)

_____ Green Gardener program at Southern Community College. You can finish
(3)

_____ Green Gardening program certificate in one year. _____ certificate is very
(4)   (5)

helpful for getting _____ job.
                    (6)

4   Mario is _____ cook. He doesn't make much _____ money. He needs to get
             (1)   (2)

_____ food safety certificate. _____ salary for cooks with _____ food safety
(3)   (4)   (5)

certificate is very good.

5   _____ architects design _____ buildings. Sometimes _____ architect works
    (1)   (2)   (3)

with _____ engineer. They solve _____ problems together.
     (4)   (5)

C Write the first draft

Now it's time to write the first draft of two pieces of writing. Use your freewrites and your ideas and language from Sections I and II to help you. You can also add any other ideas that come to mind.

Writing 1 Write a first draft about a job you want to have in the future.

Writing 2 Write a first draft about a job you have or someone you know has.

III REVISING YOUR WRITING

A Expand your vocabulary

> **PHRASES WITH THE VERB WORK**
>
> You can use these phrases to talk about jobs.
>
> - *work alone / on a team*
>   I like to work quietly, so I like to **work alone**.
>
> - *work part-time / full-time*
>   Ming **works part-time** during the school year.
>
> - *work with your hands / ideas*
>   Serge builds beautiful houses. He likes to **work with his hands**.
>
> - *work inside / outside*
>   Teachers usually **work inside**.
>
> - *work with people / numbers / adults / children*
>   Hansun is very friendly, so she likes to **work with people**.

Practice 4

Work with a partner. Complete the chart below. Find three jobs from the *Vocabulary Pool* for each *work* phrase. Then discuss your choices with your classmates.

How People Work	Jobs
1 alone	
2 on a team	
3 with their hands	
4 with ideas	
5 with people	
6 with numbers	
7 outside	
8 inside	

Practice 5

Fill in the blanks with *work* phrases from the box on page 106.

1 Accountants _____*work with numbers*_____ in their jobs.

2 I don't like to _____ during the winter.

3 Mako _____ in the mornings, but in the afternoons, he meets with the other people on the team.

4 In the summer, many people want to _____ in the sunshine.

5 Claudia makes lots of things. She really likes to _____.

6 Antonio is intelligent. He likes to _____ and solve problems.

7 Carlo loves to _____, so he works in a day-care center.

8 Engineers often _____ because they work on very large projects.

Your turn ↶

Look at your first draft of Writing 1 and Writing 2. On each draft, add at least one sentence using a *work* phrase. Remember to mark where these sentences go.

B Connect your ideas

USING BECAUSE AND SO

You can use *because* and *so* to give reasons or explain. Put *because* at the beginning of a cause/reason phrase.

   I want to be a doctor **because** I like to help people.
                                          cause / reason

Put *so* at the beginning of a result phrase. Use a comma before *so*.

   I want to help people, **so** I want to be a doctor.
                                 result

   I like to work with animals, **so** I want to be a veterinarian.
                                           result

Note: Don't use *because* and *so* in the same sentence.

Practice 6

Complete the sentences by matching cause/reason and result phrases. Add commas where necessary. Check your answers with a partner.

__e__ 1 Georgio works very hard,

_____ 2 My friend is a good teacher

_____ 3 Suk loves sports

_____ 4 Everyone loves Kaori's cooking

_____ 5 Jon wants to be a Web designer

_____ 6 Zeke wants to work only part-time

_____ 7 Jennifer is a great Web designer

_____ 8 Thomas loves biology

a so she wants to be a high school coach.

b because he likes computers.

c because he takes care of his children in the afternoons.

d so he wants to be a doctor.

e so he is always tired.

f so she wants to be a chef.

g because he is very patient.

h because she is extremely creative.

Practice 7

Read these sentences and circle the correct word. Add commas where necessary.

I love clothes and makeup, because /(so) I want to work with fashion. I want
(1)
to be a fashion designer because / so I like to draw and I like to make things
(2)
look nice. Fashion designers work with their hands and with ideas. They work
alone and they work on teams. They make new and different things because / so
(3)
they are very creative people. New clothes and styles make people happy
because / so people like to look different. Creating new styles is fun and
(4)
exciting because / so I want to be a fashion designer.
(5)

Your turn ↵

Look at your first draft of Writing 1 and Writing 2. On each draft, add sentences with *so* or *because*. Remember to mark where these sentences go.

C Give and get feedback

Work with a partner. Follow these steps to give and get feedback.

1 Show your partner your first draft of Writing 1 and Writing 2 with the sentences you added to them.

2 Exchange books. Answer the questions in the chart below about your partner's pieces of writing.

	Writing 1	Writing 2
How many words from the *Vocabulary Pool* did your partner use?		
How many count and non-count nouns did your partner use?		
How many articles did your partner use?		
How many phrases with the verb *work* did your partner use?		
How many sentences are there with *because* or *so*?		

3 What do you like about each of your partner's pieces of writing? Underline two or three parts. Tell your partner.

4 Show your partner the chart. Discuss your answers. Do you have any suggestions for your partner?

5 Return your partner's book.

D Write the second draft

Follow these steps to write the second draft.

1 Look at the chart your partner completed for your first draft of Writing 1 and Writing 2. Think about what your partner said. Did your partner give you any ideas you can use? For example, can you add any more sentences with *work* phrases?

2 Look at the *Progress Check* on page 98 of Chapter 6. Use it to help you revise your first draft of Writing 1 and Writing 2.

3 Rewrite each draft with the changes.

A Focus on mechanics

> ### FRAGMENTS
>
> A fragment is an incomplete sentence. Look at these examples.
>
>   I want to be a gardener. <u>Because I like to work outside.</u>
>
>   I like children. <u>So I want to be a teacher.</u>
>
> The first sentence in each pair is correct. The second is a fragment. It belongs with the first sentence. Remember to keep the cause/reason phrase and the result phrase in the same sentence.
>
> To fix a fragment, remove the period and combine the sentences.
>
>   I want to be a gardener because I like to work outside.
>
>   I like children, so I want to be a teacher.

Practice 8

Correct the following fragments. Cross out periods and add commas where necessary. Draw lines through capital letters and rewrite them to make them lowercase.

1 Bao doesn't like to organize things. So he doesn't want to be a manager.

2 Mya likes to work with food. So she wants to be a chef.

3 Soraida wants to become a kindergarten teacher. Because she loves children.

4 Nali is a talented artist. So she draws pictures for books.

5 Yuta doesn't want to be a gardener. Because he doesn't like to get dirty.

Practice 9

Work with a partner. Read the following fragments. Think of a cause/reason phrase or a result phrase to add to each fragment. Write the phrase in the blank and change the punctuation.

1 _____. So she wants to be a fashion designer.

2 _____. Because he likes to build things.

3 _____. So I want to be a doctor.

4 _____. Because he likes to work with computers.

5 _____. Because he likes animals.

Your turn ⤴

Check your second draft of Writing 1 and Writing 2 for fragments.

B Check for common mistakes

MISTAKES WITH ARTICLES

Articles are very difficult in English, so students often make mistakes with them.

- Use *a/an* when you don't need to be specific.

    I want to be ~~the~~ *a* landscape designer or ~~the~~ *an* architect.

- Don't use *a/an* with non-count nouns.

    Home health aides give ~~an~~ information to patients.

- Don't use an article when talking about something in a very general way.

    Nurses assist ~~the~~ doctors.

Practice 10

Read the sentences. Cross out eight more mistakes and write the corrections above them.

¹My friend is ~~the~~ *a* home health aide because she likes to help the people. ²She also likes to work indoors. ³The home health aides work in a people's homes. ⁴They work with elderly people. ⁵The home health aides prepare a healthy food for them. ⁶They give a medicine, and sometimes they give an advice. ⁷My friend cares about people, so she is the good home health aide.

C Edit your writing

Use the *Editing Checklist* below to edit your sentences. Look for only one kind of mistake each time you read your sentences. For example, the first time you read your sentences, ask yourself, "Does every sentence start with a capital letter?"

EDITING CHECKLIST ☑

- ☐ 1 Does every sentence start with a capital letter?
- ☐ 2 Does every sentence end with a period?
- ☐ 3 Did you spell all your words correctly, including plural forms of nouns?
- ☐ 4 Did you use the correct article?
- ☐ 5 Is there a variety of *work* phrases?
- ☐ 6 Are sentences with *because* or *so* complete (not fragments)?
- ☐ 7 Is there a comma in a sentence with *so*?

D Write the final draft

Make all your changes on your second draft of Writing 1 and Writing 2. Remember to mark where the changes go. Rewrite each draft. Make any changes that you need. This time, type your drafts on a computer.

V FOLLOWING UP

A Share your writing

Follow these steps to share your writing.

1 Your teacher will divide the class into Group A and Group B. The people in Group A post Writing 1 on the wall and stand next to it. The people in Group B walk around and read each piece of writing.

2 The people in Group B choose one job that they are each interested in. They talk with the writer about why they are interested in that job. For example, "I also want to be a veterinarian because I like animals."

3 Exchange roles.

B Check your progress

After you get your writing back from your teacher, complete the *Progress Check* below.

PROGRESS CHECK
Date: _____
New vocabulary I used: _____
_____
_____
New grammar I used: _____
_____
Connecting words I used: _____
Mechanics I learned: _____
Things I need to remember the next time I write: _____
_____

Important Life Events

Think about your life. What are the important events in your past? Where were you born? Where did you go to school? Who are the important people in your life and when did you meet them?

In this chapter, you write a paragraph about important events in your life.

A Useful vocabulary

Follow these steps to study words and phrases to use when you write about the important events in your life.

1 Work with a partner. Talk about the words in the *Vocabulary Pool*. Together, check (✓) the words you both know, and highlight the ones you don't know.

VOCABULARY POOL

be born	get divorced	have children
break up with	get engaged	immigrate
change jobs	get married	learn to drive
die	get promoted	lose a job
fall in love	get remarried	meet someone
finish school	get sick	move
get a degree	go to college	quit a job
get a job	go to school	retire
get a pet	graduate	start school
get a scholarship	grow up	

2 Change partners. Look at your new partner's highlighted words. Explain them to your partner if you can.

3 With your partner, complete the chart with words from the *Vocabulary Pool*. Some words go into more than one category. Then compare with another pair.

General Life	Relationships	Learning	Work
be born	get married	learn to drive	get a job

4 Check (✓) the things in the chart that happened in your life. Then tell your partner about the important events in your life.

B Vocabulary in context

Follow these steps to use and read words and phrases from the *Vocabulary Pool*.

- With a partner, talk about the life events in each picture.
- Read the paragraphs. Talk about when the life events in the picture happened.
- Put the letters of the picture in the correct places on each time line.

1 Francisco's Life

Francisco was born in 1985 in Brazil. His father died two years later. After many years, he and his mother got visas and immigrated to the United States. Then he immediately started high school. He wanted to go to college, so he studied hard and got good grades. At 15, he got a job. At 16, he got his driver's license. A year later, he got a car. Francisco graduated one year after that. He also won a scholarship. Then he had enough money to go to college! A year later, he moved to New York and started classes.

1985	1987	1999	2000	2001	2002	2003	2004
born	father died	_____ (1) then started school	got a job	_____ (2)	_____ (3)	_____ (4) and won a scholarship	_____ (5) and started classes

2 My Life

I was born in Taiwan in 1983. I graduated from high school 18 years later. I didn't want to go to college, so after high school, I traveled for a while. Then, after a year, I found a job in an office. I worked as an administrative assistant for four years. During those four years, I gradually started to change my mind about college. I finally applied to college. In 2006, I started classes. In my second year of college, I met Il Suk. We fell in love, but we broke up once. We got married two years after we met.

1983	2001	2002	2005	2006	2008	2009	2010
born	graduated high school and _____ (1)	_____ (2)	applied to college	_____ (3)	_____ (4)	broke up	_____ (5)

C Get ideas

Follow these steps to get ideas to write about important life events.

1 Put at least five of the important events of your life on this time line. Use words from the *Vocabulary Pool*. Write dates above each event.

born

2 Work with a partner. Tell your partner about the events on your time line. Ask questions about your partner's time line.

3 Did your partner put any events that you can use for your time line? Add those events to your time line.

D Freewrite

Now it's time to freewrite about your life and the important events on your time line. Write everything that you think of, and don't worry about grammar or spelling. You can write words, phrases, and sentences. Don't stop to erase anything. Just keep writing until your teacher tells you to stop.

A Learn about the simple past

> ### THE SIMPLE PAST
>
> Use the simple past to talk about things people did in the past.
>
> > Six years ago, Ana **started** college and **studied** English. She **graduated** four years later. Then she **traveled** all over Europe, but she **stopped** in France. She **lived** there for one year.
>
> Follow these rules to form the simple past.
>
> - Add *-ed* to regular verbs to form the simple past. Just add *-d* to regular verbs that end in *-e*.
>
>   start → start**ed**
>
>   graduate → graduate**d**
>
> - If a verb ends in a consonant + *-y*, change the *-y* to *-i* and then add *-ed*.
>
>   study → stud**ied**
>
> - If a verb has one syllable and ends in one consonant, double the consonant and then add *-ed*.
>
>   stop → stop**ped**
>
> For more rules about adding *-ed*, see Appendix F on page 166.

Practice 1

Fill in the blanks with the past form of the verb in parentheses.

1 Last summer, my brother and I _____ (walk) across the Brooklyn Bridge.

2 I _____ (work) in a restaurant during high school.

3 My family _____ (live) on a farm in the country for one year.

4 Last year, Uncle Wei _____ (immigrate) to the United States.

5 Sam and Emilio _____ (move) to Florida in 2007.

6 During high school, Mei _____ (carry) a lucky stone with her everywhere.

7 He _____ (plan) the trip years ago.

8 They _____ (play) at the Mercury Club for 10 years.

9 They _____ (finish) school a long time ago.

10 Two years ago, my grandparents _____ (travel) all over the world.

TIME EXPRESSIONS WITH THE SIMPLE PAST

We often use time expressions with the simple past. Here are some common time expressions.

- *in* + year

  In 1999, Bao moved to the United States.

- *last* week / month / year / spring / summer / fall / winter

  I graduated from high school **last year**.

- [number] days / months / years / a long time *ago*

  Solange immigrated to Canada **two years ago**.

- [number] days / months / years *later*

  I graduated in 2005. I started college **one year later**.

- *for* + period of time

  Claudia played soccer **for five years**.

Remember to use a comma when the time expression comes at the beginning of the sentence.

Practice 2

On a separate piece of paper, put these words in the right order. If the time expression begins with a capital letter, put it at the beginning of the sentence and use a comma. When you finish, write the sentences in a paragraph.

1 to Hawaii / in 1956 / Lee immigrated / from Taiwan
2 He / a long time ago / learned English
3 for four years / He / at a community college / took classes
4 at the University of Hawaii / he started / Two years later
5 Lee / from the University of Hawaii / graduated / In 1982
6 he worked / From 1982 to 1992 / in Honolulu / at a bank
7 10 years ago / to Philadelphia / Lee moved
8 a business / Four years later / Lee started
9 Lee earned / For many years / a lot of money
10 Last year / of hard work / after many years / Lee retired

Practice 3

Read Rob's time line. Then complete the story with the correct time expression below. Use each time expression only once.

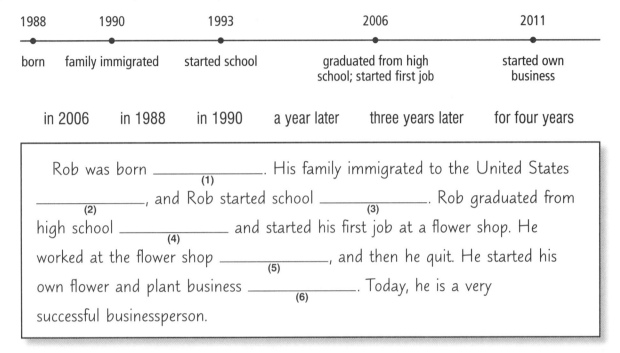

1988	1990	1993	2006	2011
born	family immigrated	started school	graduated from high school; started first job	started own business

in 2006   in 1988   in 1990   a year later   three years later   for four years

Rob was born _____(1)_____. His family immigrated to the United States _____(2)_____, and Rob started school _____(3)_____. Rob graduated from high school _____(4)_____ and started his first job at a flower shop. He worked at the flower shop _____(5)_____, and then he quit. He started his own flower and plant business _____(6)_____. Today, he is a very successful businessperson.

B Learn more about the simple past

SIMPLE PAST – IRREGULAR VERBS

Many verbs have an irregular past tense form. Some common irregular verbs are *go, do, have, make,* and *get.*

I **went** to school in Costa Rica for four years.

We **did** our homework at the library last night.

They **had** a lot of fun last summer.

My grandfather **made** furniture many years ago.

Marta **got** a job in New York City.

We often use *get* + verb to talk about many life events. To describe these events in the past, use *got* + verb.

Ravi **got promoted** last week. Now he is a manager.

Sid and Sara **got married** in 2001, but they **got divorced** in 2002.

Here are some more common verbs that have irregular past tense forms.

become → became	begin → began	grow up → grew up
meet → met	lose → lost	win → won

For more irregular past tense forms, see Appendix D on page 164.

Note: *Was / Were born* is a special expression in English.

I **was born** in 1995. My parents **were born** a long time go.

Practice 4

Complete the story with the past form of the verbs in parentheses.

Lorena Ochoa _____ (be born) in 1981. She _____ (grow up)
(1)   (2)
in Guadalajara, Mexico. She _____ (start) playing golf at the age of
(3)
five. She _____ (win) a state competition at the age of six, and a
(4)
national competition at the age of seven. Ochoa _____ (attend) the
(5)
University of Arizona. She _____ (play) in 20 college competitions and
(6)
_____ (lost) only 8 times. Ochoa _____ (become) a professional
(7)   (8)
golfer in 2002. She _____ (have) many successful competitions. In
(9)
2008, she _____ (win) the Corona Championship in Mexico. After
(10)
that, she _____ (enter) the World Golf Hall of Fame. Ochoa wanted to
(11)
help young people become golfers, so she _____ (start) a scholarship
(12)
program for young Mexican golfers.

SIMPLE PAST – NEGATIVE

Use *didn't* + the base form of the verb to talk about things that didn't happen in
the past.

He **didn't grow up** in the United States.

They **didn't graduate** from high school.

Practice 5

Answer the questions below. Write complete sentences.

1 What didn't you do this morning?

I didn't go to the gym this morning.

2 What didn't you do five years ago?

_____

3 What didn't you do last weekend?

_____

4 What didn't you do last year?

_____

5 What didn't you do in your childhood?

_____

C Learn about paragraphs

ONE PARAGRAPH = ONE IDEA

A paragraph is a group of sentences about one idea. For example, this paragraph is about Duke Kahanamoku. He is a famous swimmer and surfer. However, notice that this paragraph is only about Kahanamoku's achievements as a swimmer. His achievements as a surfer belong in a different paragraph.

> Duke Kahanamoku is famous for his surfing, but he was also an Olympic swimmer. He was born in Honolulu in 1890. During his childhood, Kahanamoku learned how to swim. In 1911, he competed in a swimming competition. He won that competition. He also broke a world speed record in that competition. He competed in the 1912 Olympics in Sweden and won a gold medal and a silver medal. Then Kahanamoku competed in the 1920 Olympics and the 1924 Olympics. He won many more medals for swimming. He participated in the 1932 Olympics in Los Angeles, but he didn't win any medals. After that, he retired from Olympic competition.

Practice 6

The two lists of sentences below come from two paragraphs. Some of the sentences do not belong with the other sentences. Write an X next to the sentences that do not belong.

List A

_____ Barack Obama was born in Hawaii.

_____ His father left when he was two years old.

_____ He moved to Indonesia with his mother when he was six years old.

_____ Indonesian is a difficult language to learn.

_____ He moved back to Hawaii when he was 10.

_____ He went to Punahou School in Hawaii.

_____ Punahou is very expensive and very large.

_____ He graduated in 1979.

List B

_____ My brother Ji-Sek is a great violinist.

_____ We shared a bedroom.

_____ I was born in 1987.

_____ He started playing the violin when he was only five years old.

_____ He is very good at the violin.

_____ He played with the city orchestra when he was a teen.

_____ He is very smart.

Practice 7

Reread the two lists of sentences from *Practice 6*. Then read the ideas below. Circle the idea that best describes each list of sentences.

List A

a Barack Obama

b Obama in Indonesia

c Obama's childhood

List B

a Ji-Sek's education

b Ji-Sek, a great violinist

c My younger brother

Your turn ∿

Look back at your freewrite. Choose one part of your life to write about. On a piece of paper, make a list of possible topics. For example:

My education

My childhood

My teen years

My professional life

My life with my boyfriend/girlfriend or husband/wife

Then make a list of the important events for your topic. For example:

Topic:

My childhood

Events:

broke my leg

met my best friend

started at a new school

D Write the first draft

Now it's time to write the first draft. Write about your life. Use your freewrite, your *Your turn* notes, and your ideas and language from Sections I and II to help you. You can also add any other ideas that come to mind.

III REVISING YOUR WRITING

A Expand your vocabulary

> **MORE ADVERBS**
>
> In Chapter 5, you learned that adverbs can describe how often an action happens. Adverbs can also describe how much time an action takes.
>
> - Use *eventually*, *finally*, *gradually*, or *slowly* for actions that took a lot of time.
>   I started college in 1995. I **eventually** got my degree in 2001.
>   School wasn't easy for me. I studied for a long time. **Finally,** I graduated from college.
>   I studied English for 10 years. I **gradually** learned how to speak and write in English.
>   I worked for many years. **Slowly,** I saved enough money for school.
>
> - Use *quickly* or *immediately* for actions that took very little time.
>   I had a good teacher, so I **quickly** learned how to drive.
>   I liked my husband right away. We **immediately** fell in love!
>
> Note: Use a comma when these words come at the beginning of the sentence.

Practice 8

Read the sentences. Circle the correct adverb. Add commas, if necessary.

1 I met Carlos in high school in Chile. We were friends for many years. I liked him and he liked me, and we *gradually / immediately* fell in love.

2 After high school, we both went to the university. We studied for many years. *Immediately / Finally* we got our degrees.

3 *Quickly / Finally* after many years, we got married.

4 Then we tried to find jobs. It wasn't very difficult. We *slowly / quickly* found jobs.

5 We always wanted to see the United States, so we saved our money for a long time. We *eventually / quickly* saved enough money for the trip.

6 One day, we went to the Grand Canyon and the desert. We were amazed! We *slowly / immediately* fell in love with Arizona!

7 We wanted to come back to Arizona soon, so we *finally / quickly* quit our jobs and moved to the United States.

Your turn ↰

Look at your first draft. Add at least three sentences with an adverb from the box above. Remember to mark where these sentences go.

B Connect your ideas

USING THEN, NEXT, AND AFTER THAT

You can use *then*, *next*, and *after that* to show the order of events.

I graduated from high school in 2005. **Then** I came to the United States.

Aisha got a job. **Next,** she applied for a scholarship.

Lorena Ochoa won the Corona Championship. **After that,** she entered the World Golf Hall of Fame.

Use a comma with *next* and *after that*.

Note: Don't overuse ordering words. Not every sentence in your paragraph needs an ordering word.

Practice 9

Read about Lang Lang's life. Add *then*, *next*, and *after that* to show the order of events. Use each word or phrase at least once. Change capital letters and add commas where necessary.

¹Lang Lang is a famous Chinese pianist. ²He began piano lessons at the age of three. ³*Then* h~~He~~ won the Shenyang Piano Competition at the age of five. ⁴Lang Lang entered Beijing's Central Music Conservatory. ⁵He won an important music award at the age of 11. ⁶He studied at the Curtis Institute in Philadelphia. ⁷Lang Lang played with the Los Angeles Symphony at 17. ⁸He performed at London's Royal Albert Hall in 2003.

Your turn

Look at your first draft. Add at least three sentences with *then*, *next*, or *after that*. Remember to mark where these sentences go.

C Give and get feedback

Work with a partner. Follow these steps to give and get feedback.

1 Show your partner your first draft with the sentences you added to it.

2 Exchange books. Answer the questions in the chart below about your partner's piece of writing.

	Your Partner's Writing
How many words from the *Vocabulary Pool* did your partner use?	
How many sentences are in the simple past?	
How many irregular past tense forms did your partner use?	
How many sentences are in the negative simple past?	
This paragraph is about: _____ **(idea)** How many sentences are *not* about this idea?	
How many sentences have adverbs?	
How many sentences use *then*, *next*, and *after that*?	

3 What do you like about your partner's piece of writing? Underline two or three parts. Tell your partner.

4 Show your partner the chart. Discuss your answers. Do you have any suggestions for your partner?

5 Return your partner's book.

D Write the second draft

Follow these steps to write the second draft.

1 Look at the chart your partner completed for your first draft. Think about what your partner said. Did your partner give you any ideas you can use? For example, can you add any more sentences with *then*, *next*, and *after that*?

2 Check that your paragraph is about only one idea.

3 Look at the *Progress Check* on page 112 of Chapter 7. Use it to help you revise your first draft.

4 Rewrite your paragraph with the changes.

A Focus on mechanics

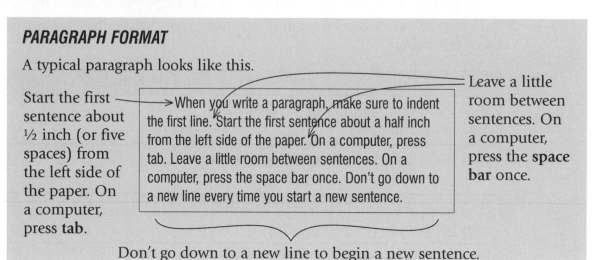

PARAGRAPH FORMAT

A typical paragraph looks like this.

Start the first sentence about ½ inch (or five spaces) from the left side of the paper. On a computer, press **tab**.

When you write a paragraph, make sure to indent the first line. Start the first sentence about a half inch from the left side of the paper. On a computer, press tab. Leave a little room between sentences. On a computer, press the space bar once. Don't go down to a new line every time you start a new sentence.

Leave a little room between sentences. On a computer, press the **space bar** once.

Don't go down to a new line to begin a new sentence.

Practice 10

Read this paragraph and number the sentences. Then find the formatting mistakes below. Write the sentence numbers on the lines.

My great-grandfather had an interesting life. He was born in Moscow, Russia, in 1875. At 14, he moved to the United States.

He started working immediately.

He found pieces of glass on the street and sold them to factories.

At 19, he started a small glass business.Three years later, he met my great-grandmother. They got married in 1899. After that, the glass business grew.My great-grandfather became very rich.

My great-grandfather died in 1965.He had a long and happy life.

1 The writer didn't leave one space between sentences. ____ and ____, ____ and ____, ____ and ____

2 The writer went down to a new line to begin a new sentence. ____ ____ ____ ____

3 The writer didn't start the first sentence a few spaces from the left. ____

Your turn 〰

Check your paragraph formatting in your second draft. Remember to mark where any changes go.

B Check for common mistakes

> ### MISTAKES WITH THE SIMPLE PAST
>
> Many students make mistakes with the simple past. If an action happened in the past, make sure the verb has a past tense ending. If there are two or more verbs in a sentence about the past, make sure both verbs are in the past tense.
>
>   *moved*
> Last year, I graduated from high school and ~~move~~ to the city.
>
> The past tense of irregular verbs do not end in -ed.
>
>   *grew*
> He ~~growed~~ up in Singapore.
>
> In negative sentences, use *didn't* + base form of the verb.
>
>   *graduate*
> They didn't ~~graduated~~ from high school last year.

Practice 11

Read the paragraph. Cross out six more mistakes and write the corrections above them.

---

                                         died

¹My wife was born in 1980. ²Her parents ~~die~~ two years later. ³She goed to live with her grandparents. ⁴She graduated high school in 1998, and then she start college. ⁵She didn't finished college. ⁶After two years, she needed money, so she stop. ⁷She get a job in an office. ⁸I also worked in that office. ⁹We married two years later and buy a big house.

C Edit your writing

Use the *Editing Checklist* below to edit your paragraph. Look for only one kind of mistake each time you read your sentences. For example, the first time you read your sentences, ask yourself, "Does every sentence start with a capital letter?"

> ### EDITING CHECKLIST ☑
>
> ☐ **1** Does every sentence start with a capital letter?
>
> ☐ **2** Does every sentence end with a period?
>
> ☐ **3** Did you spell all your words correctly?
>
> ☐ **4** Did you indent the first line of your paragraph?
>
> ☐ **5** Did you use the correct past tense forms?
>
> ☐ **6** Did you use commas after time words when they came at the beginning of sentences?

D Write the final draft

Make all your changes on your second draft. Remember to mark where the changes go. This time, type your paragraph on a computer. Make any changes that you need.

V FOLLOWING UP

A Share your writing

Follow these steps to share your writing.

1 On a separate piece of paper, make a time line for your life story. Don't use any names.
2 Give your life story and your time line to your teacher.
3 Get into groups of 10 or 12 students. Your teacher will give half of your group time lines and the other half life stories. Read the life story or the time line.
4 Stand up and ask questions to find the student who has the matching life story or time line. Do not show each other your story or your time line.
5 When you have found your match, sit down and compare the time line with the life story.
6 Repeat this process with the other half of the time lines and life stories for your group.

B Check your progress

After you get your writing back from your teacher, complete the *Progress Check* below.

```
┌─────────────────────────────────────────────────────────────┐
│                      PROGRESS CHECK                           │
├─────────────────────────────────────────────────────────────┤
│                                                               │
│   Date: _____                          │
│   New vocabulary I used: _____ │
│   _____ │
│   _____ │
│                                                               │
│   New grammar I used: _____ │
│   _____ │
│                                                               │
│   New paragraph skills I learned: _____ │
│   _____ │
│                                                               │
│   Connecting words I used: _____ │
│   Mechanics I learned: _____ │
│   Things I need to remember the next time I write: _____ │
│   _____ │
└─────────────────────────────────────────────────────────────┘
```

Going Places

Think about a trip you took in the past. Where did you go? How was the trip? What was the place you visited like? What did you do there? What was the weather like?

In this chapter, you write a paragraph about a trip you once took.

A Useful vocabulary

Follow these steps to study words to use when you write about trips.

1 Work with a partner. Talk about the words in the *Vocabulary Pool*. Together, check (✓) the words you both know, and highlight the ones you don't know.

VOCABULARY POOL

boring	expensive	popular
busy	fascinating	quiet
cheap	filthy	relaxing
cheerful	fun	safe
colorful	historic	stressful
crowded	horrible	terrible
dangerous	lovely	tiring
depressing	noisy	touristy
enjoyable	peaceful	ugly
exciting	pleasant	uncomfortable

2 Change partners. Look at your new partner's highlighted words. Explain them to your partner if you can.

3 Find words in the *Vocabulary Pool* that you can use to describe good things and bad things about a trip. Complete the chart below. Then compare your answers with a partner.

Good Things	Bad Things
enjoyable	*depressing*

4 Get into groups. Describe a trip you took in the past. Think about the food, the weather, the cost, and so on. Talk about the good parts and the bad parts of the trip. Use words from the *Vocabulary Pool*.

B Vocabulary in context

Follow these steps to use and read words from the *Vocabulary Pool*.

- With a partner, describe each picture.
- Read the paragraphs. Match the paragraphs to the pictures. Write the numbers of the paragraphs in the box on each picture.
- Find good things and bad things that happened during each trip. Add them to the chart on the right.

1   We took a trip to Singapore last summer. As soon as we got there, we went shopping. The clothes in Singapore were very cheap, so we bought a lot of new things. We also went to a lot of museums. They were fascinating. My favorite museum was the art museum. We spent all day there. After we went to the museum, we were very tired. We also went to a lot of wonderful restaurants. The food was delicious, but it was spicy. Our hotel had a great pool. We swam every day before we went out. The weather wasn't very nice. It was extremely hot, and it rained every afternoon. However, we still had a great time.

Good Things
Bad Things

2   I took the train to Chicago with my friends last weekend. We stayed in a small hotel. It was fairly cheap, but it wasn't bad. After we arrived, we went for a walk downtown on the Miracle Mile. The buildings were very beautiful, but it was extremely crowded. We looked in the beautiful stores. However, things were very expensive, so we didn't buy anything. After that, we went back to our hotel and took a nap. In the evening we went to some clubs. The music was great, but it was extremely loud. The next day, we woke up late, and we all had headaches. We had breakfast in the hotel. However, it wasn't very good. When we finished, we took the train home. It was a good weekend.

Good Things
Bad Things

C Get ideas

Follow these steps to get ideas to write about trips.

1 Work with a partner. Talk about trips that you took in the past.
2 Work alone. Complete the chart with where you went, and the good things that happened and the bad things that happened.

Trip To . . .	Good Things	Bad Things

3 Work with a new partner. Tell each other about your trips.
4 Did your partner use any words that you can use? Add them to your chart.

D Freewrite

Now it's time to freewrite about trips you took in the past. Write everything that you think of, and don't worry about grammar or spelling. You can write words, phrases, and sentences. Don't stop to erase anything. Just keep writing until your teacher tells you to stop.

A Learn about the simple past of *be*

> ### USING THE SIMPLE PAST OF BE
>
> *Be* is an irregular verb. The simple past forms are *was* and *were*.
>
>   I **was** uncomfortable on the plane.
>
>   The restaurants **were** expensive, but the food **was** good.
>
>   There **were** several tourists in our hotel, so it **was** noisy.
>
> The negative past forms of *be* are *was not* and *were not*. We often use the contractions *wasn't* and *weren't* with these forms.
>
>   The museum **wasn't** near our hotel, but the buses **weren't** expensive.

Practice 1

Read the following sentences about a trip someone took. Complete the sentences with the correct form of *be*.

1 The people at the hotel _____ (not be) very helpful.

2 The shops _____ (be) small, but there _____ (be) a lot to buy.

3 We _____ (be) very lucky because the weather _____ (be) great.

4 The food _____ (be) expensive, and it _____ (not be) very good.

5 The beach _____ (not be) crowded, and the water _____ (be) warm.

6 My arm _____ (be) tired because my suitcase _____ (be) heavy.

Practice 2

Complete the paragraph with the correct forms of the verbs in parentheses.

> Last summer, my family and I _____ (go) to San Diego. It _____ (be)
> (1)   (2)
> a great trip because there _____ (be) a lot to do. We _____ (go) to the
> (3)   (4)
> museums in Balboa Park. They _____ (be) all very interesting, but the Air and
> (5)
> Space Museum _____ (be) my favorite museum. There _____ (be) a
> (6)   (7)
> model of Lindbergh's plane. I _____ (be) amazed! We also _____ (go) to
> (8)   (9)
> the beach. There _____ (not be) very many people at the beach, so it
> (10)
> _____ (be) nice. We _____ (watch) the surfers for a while. We
> (11)   (12)
> _____ (not go) in the water because it _____ (not be) very warm.
> (13)   (14)
> However, the weather _____ (be) great. The sun _____ (be) out every day.
> (15)   (16)

B Learn about clauses

USING BEFORE, WHEN, AND AFTER IN CLAUSES

You can use *before*, *when*, and *after* to show the order of two events in time.

I read several travel guides **before** I visited Singapore.

I ate lots of spicy food **when** I was in Singapore.

I went to Thailand **after** I left Singapore.

Notice that *before*, *when*, and *after* connect two short sentences. These small sentences within a larger sentence are called *clauses*.

I read several travel guides **before** I visited Singapore.

      clause   +   clause

You can also use *before*, *when*, and *after* clauses at the beginning of sentences. Remember to use a comma at the end of the first clause.

After I visited Singapore, I went to Thailand.

Practice 3

Read the paragraph about the Brown family's trip to Puerto Rico. Then answer the questions in complete sentences using *before*, *when*, or *after*. Make sure you use all three as many times as possible. Then compare your answers with a partner.

My family and I went to Puerto Rico last September. We stayed in a hotel on Vieques Island. It was an interesting vacation. Before we went to Puerto Rico, we read a guidebook, and we asked friends about the area. However, we didn't pay attention to information about the weather. When we arrived, the weather was beautiful. We had a lot of fun the first two days. We went to the beach, and we went sightseeing. We had wonderful seafood. On the third day, the weather changed. The sky was dark. Then we heard the news: It was hurricane season. The hurricane came that night. Before it came, we went to the grocery store and bought food and water for two days. We also bought gas for our car. There were long lines at all the stores before the hurricane hit. However, when it started, everyone went home. When the hurricane came, we were ready. We stayed indoors and had a good time. We cooked and played games. After the hurricane ended, everything was calm but very wet!

1 When did the Browns read a guidebook?

_____

2 When was the weather beautiful?

_____

3 When did the Browns go to the beach?

_____

4 When did the Browns buy food, water, and gas?

_____

5 When were there long lines at all the stores?

_____

6 When did everyone go indoors?

_____

7 When did the Browns stay indoors?

_____

8 When was everything calm?

_____

Practice 4

Read Danielle's travel diary. Write four sentences with *before*, *when*, and *after*.

Dear **Diary**

April: I applied for a passport.

May: My friend gave me a book about Italy. My passport arrived.

June 15: My friend and I went to Rome.

June 16: We arrived in Rome.

June 16–June 23: We were in Rome. We went sightseeing. We went to the National Museum. We went shopping. We ate a lot of delicious Italian food! We met some students at the university, Paolo and Mauro. We took a lot of pictures.

June 23: We arrived home.

June 24: We were very tired. We got e-mails from Paolo and Mauro!

_____

_____

_____

_____

C Learn about paragraphs

GENERAL AND SPECIFIC SENTENCES

There are two kinds of sentences in a paragraph.

- Sentences with general information
- Sentences with specific information

Specific sentences give more details about general sentences. They follow general sentences. A paragraph can sometimes have several specific sentences for each general sentence.

The following are examples of general sentences and specific sentences.

General Sentences	Specific Sentences
We stayed in a very nice hotel.	Our room was small but comfortable.
We had a lot of fun the first two days.	We went to the beach, and we went sightseeing.

Practice 5

For each general sentence on the left, find two specific sentences on the right. Write the specific sentences under the correct general sentences.

General Sentences

1 The shopping was great.

_____

_____

2 The hotel was horrible.

_____

_____

3 We ate dinner at a terrible restaurant.

_____

_____

4 We took a lot of buses.

_____

_____

5 We went to the beach almost every day.

_____

_____

Specific Sentences

They were cheap and on time.

The food was bad.

The sand was very clean.

The beds were uncomfortable.

There were lots of beautiful clothing stores.

The seats were comfortable.

The waiters were extremely rude.

The water was warm and relaxing.

The rooms were small and dark.

There were many shoe stores, too.

Your turn ⌁

Look back at your freewrite. Choose a trip to write about. In the chart, make a list of the general things you did on the trip. Then write two or three specific details about what you did.

What I Did (General Information)	Details About What I Did (Specific Information)
went sightseeing	took a tour of the city saw lots of old buildings took a lot of pictures

D Write the first draft

Now it's time to write the first draft. Write about a trip. Use your freewrite, your *Your turn* notes, and your ideas and language from Sections I and II to help you. You can also add any other ideas that come to mind.

A Expand your vocabulary

WEATHER WORDS

You can use nouns or adjectives to talk about the weather.

Noun	Adjective
We had a lot of **rain** last weekend.	It was **rainy** last weekend.
We didn't get much **snow** this year.	It wasn't very **snowy** this year.
There were a lot of **clouds** in the sky.	It was very **cloudy**.
The **sun** was very bright.	It was **sunny**.
The **wind** was very strong by the water.	It was very **windy** by the water.

We often use these weather words together.

gray and **overcast**

hot and **humid/dry**

cold and **rainy**

clear and **bright**

gray and overcast

Practice 6

Match each sentence with a sentence on the right. Discuss your answers with a partner.

_____ **1** The weather was great.

_____ **2** The weather was terrible.

_____ **3** The sky was always overcast.

_____ **4** It was extremely hot.

_____ **5** The weather was cold but beautiful.

_____ **6** It was extremely cold.

a It was 12°F (about –11°C).

b It was cloudy every day.

c It was over 100°F (about 38°C) most days.

d It was warm and sunny every day.

e It was clear and bright.

f It was rainy every day.

Practice 7

Read the paragraph. Then read it again and choose a sentence below that fits each blank.

a It was only about 30°F (–1°C).   **d** It was cold but sunny.
b It started to rain.   **e** It was very windy.
c The sky was gray and overcast.

We went to Washington, D.C., last April to see the cherry trees. The weather changed many times during our trip. When we got there, the weather was great. _____ We needed jackets, but we didn't need umbrellas. The cherry trees looked (1)
beautiful. However, when we woke up the next day, the weather was very different. It was very dark outside. _____ After we ate breakfast, we went to the (2)
park to see the trees again, but all the cherry blossoms were on the ground. _____ Suddenly, it got very cold. We went into a coffee shop. The weather (3)
changed again. _____ We stayed in the coffee shop for two hours because we (4)
didn't have our umbrellas. Finally, the rain stopped, and we went outside, but it was freezing. _____ It was cold for the rest of our trip, but we had a good time. (5)

Your turn ↻

Look at your first draft. Add at least two sentences about the weather. Remember to mark where these sentences go.

B Connect your ideas

USING HOWEVER, FOR EXAMPLE, AND BECAUSE

However connects two sentences with contrasting ideas.

We had a great trip. **However,** it was very expensive.
The people were friendly. **However,** they talked too much.

In Chapter 6, you connected two sentences with *for example*. You can use *for example* at the beginning of a sentence to give more information.

We ate at a very expensive restaurant. **For example,** a bowl of soup was $12!

In Chapter 7, you connected sentences with *because*. You can use *because* to explain or give reasons.

We didn't eat at Sammy's Café **because** it was very expensive.

Note: Don't forget to use a comma after *however* and *for example*.

Practice 8

Complete the sentences with *however*, *for example*, or *because*. Add commas where necessary.

1 I liked our trip to Santa Fe last year. _____ we stayed too long.

2 We didn't spend a lot of time at the beaches _____ it was cold.

3 We visited a lot people in Seoul. _____ we visited my grandmother, my aunt, and most of my cousins.

4 My trip to Paris was inexpensive. _____ the hotel room was only $50 a night.

5 We met a lot of nice people in Oaxaca. _____ the people in our hotel were not very nice.

6 We didn't visit the museums _____ they were very crowded.

Your turn ↶

Look at your first draft. Add at least one sentence with *however*, one with *for example*, and one with *because*. Remember to mark where these sentences go.

C Give and get feedback

Work with a partner. Follow these steps to get feedback on your writing.

1 Show your partner your first draft with the sentences you added to it.

2 Exchange books. Answer the questions in the chart below about your partner's first draft.

	Your Partner's Writing
How many words from the *Vocabulary Pool* did your partner use?	
How many sentences with the simple past of *be* are there?	
How many sentences with *before*, *when*, and *after* are there?	
How many general sentences are there?	
How many specific sentences are there?	
How many sentences about the weather are there?	
How many sentences with *however*, *for example*, and *because* are there?	

3 What do you like about your partner's piece of writing? Underline two or three parts. Tell your partner.

4 Show your partner the chart. Discuss your answers. Do you have any suggestions for your partner?

5 Return your partner's book.

D Write the second draft

Follow these steps to write the second draft.

1 Look at the chart your partner completed for your first draft. Think about what your partner said. Did your partner give you any ideas you can use? For example, can you add any more sentences with *before*, *when*, or *after*?

2 Check that your paragraph has both general and specific sentences, and that the specific sentences come after the general sentences.

3 Look at the *Progress Check* on page 128 of Chapter 8. Use it to help you revise your first draft.

4 Rewrite your paragraph with the changes.

IV EDITING YOUR WRITING

A Focus on mechanics

USING COMMAS WITH TIME WORDS, EXPRESSIONS, AND CLAUSES

Use commas when these words, phrases, and clauses begin a sentence.

- Time words

  Eventually, the plane took off.

- Time expressions

  Two hours later, the air-conditioning broke.

- Time clauses

  Before I went to Seoul, I didn't like Korean food.

Don't use commas when the time words, expressions, and clauses come at the end of the sentence.

The plane took off **eventually**.

The air-conditioning broke **two hours later**.

I didn't like Korean food **before I went to Seoul**.

Practice 9

Read the paragraph and underline the time words, expressions, and clauses. Then put commas in the right places. Check your answers with a partner.

> ¹Last July we went to San Francisco for our vacation. ²Before we left we packed our suitcases. ³We packed lots of shorts, T-shirts, and sandals. ⁴After that we went to the airport. ⁵When we got to the airport we checked our bags and went to the gate. ⁶The flight was late. ⁷We waited at the gate for four hours! ⁸Finally our plane took off. ⁹We arrived in San Francisco very late at night. ¹⁰After we arrived we went to get our suitcases, but they weren't there. ¹¹They were lost! ¹²We filled out a lot of forms at the airport. ¹³It was midnight! ¹⁴Finally we left the airport. ¹⁵We took the subway, but we got lost. ¹⁶About two hours later we found our hotel. ¹⁷When we woke up the next day our suitcases were at the hotel. ¹⁸We were happy. ¹⁹However, the weather was terrible! ²⁰It was cold and rainy every day, so we bought some warm clothes!

Your turn ↶

Look at your second draft. Check your use of commas.

B Check for common mistakes

> **FORMING THE SIMPLE PAST**
>
> Students sometimes make mistakes with the simple past tense; they use the past tense of *be* with another verb. You can use the past tense of *be* or the past tense of another verb. You cannot use both.
>
> I was ~~go~~ in Peru last month.
>
> They ~~were walk~~ to work this morning. *(walked)*
>
> I wasn't ~~go~~ in Peru last month.
>
> They ~~weren't~~ walk to work this morning. *(didn't)*

Practice 10

Read this paragraph. Cross out five mistakes with the simple past. Write the corrections above the mistakes.

> ¹Two years ago, we were climb Mt. Fuji in Japan. ²Before we were go, we read a lot of books. ³We packed all the right clothes. ⁴We were take bottles of water and lots of snacks. ⁵They were really heavy! ⁶When we were get to the mountain, we saw a lot of snack bars. ⁷We weren't need all our food!

C Edit your writing

Use the *Editing Checklist* below to edit your paragraph. Look for only one kind of mistake each time you read your sentences. For example, the first time you read your sentences, ask yourself, "Does every sentence start with a capital letter?"

EDITING CHECKLIST ☑

- ☐ **1** Does every sentence start with a capital letter?
- ☐ **2** Does every sentence end with a period?
- ☐ **3** Did you spell all your words correctly?
- ☐ **4** Did you indent the first line of your paragraph?
- ☐ **5** Did you start new sentences in the correct place?
- ☐ **6** Did you leave a space between your sentences?
- ☐ **7** Did you use the correct past forms?
- ☐ **8** Did you use commas after time words, expressions, and clauses that come at the beginning of a sentence?

D Write the final draft

Make all your changes on your second draft. Remember to mark where the changes go. This time, type your paragraph on a computer. Make any changes that you need.

A Share your writing

Follow these steps to share your writing.

1 Get into small groups.
2 Exchange paragraphs and read about each other's trips.
3 Rate each trip on a scale of 1 to 5, where "5" is a trip you want to take, and "1" is a trip you are not interested in taking. Circle a number for each trip.

Trip:	1	2	3	4	5
Trip:	1	2	3	4	5
Trip:	1	2	3	4	5
Trip:	1	2	3	4	5
Trip:	1	2	3	4	5

4 Now pass your classmate's paper to another student and read the next paper.
5 Rate that trip, and repeat the process until you are finished reading all the papers.
6 Compare charts and give reasons for your ratings.

B Check your progress

After you get your writing back from your teacher, complete the *Progress Check* below.

PROGRESS CHECK

Date: _____

New vocabulary I used: _____

_____

_____

New grammar I used: _____

_____

New paragraph skills I learned: _____

_____

Connecting words I used: _____

Mechanics I learned: _____

Things I need to remember the next time I write: _____

_____

In the Future

Think about your future. What are your plans? Are you going to get a degree? Do you expect to change jobs? Do you hope to get married? Do you plan to have children? Do you want to travel?

In this chapter, you write a paragraph about your future plans.

A Useful vocabulary

Follow these steps to study words and phrases to use when you write about future plans.

1 Look through the *Getting Started* sections of Chapters 2, 3, 4, 7, and 8. Find words and phrases to use to talk about possible future plans. Write them in the *Vocabulary Pool*. Then add words and phrases of your own.

VOCABULARY POOL

> *change jobs*
> *get married*

2 Use the words and phrases from your *Vocabulary Pool* to complete the chart below.

Personal Life	Education	Career/Job	Other Future Plans
get married		change jobs	

3 Work with a partner. Compare charts. Did your partner use any words that you can use? Add them to your chart.

B Vocabulary in context

Follow these steps to use and read words and phrases from the *Vocabulary Pool*.

- Look at the pictures and make guesses about the people's possible future plans.
- Read the paragraphs below. Match the people with their plans. Write the letter of the picture on the line. You will not use one letter.
- Talk about the amount of time each plan needs. Are the plans short-term (less than two years) or long-term (2–40 years)? Circle *short-term* or *long-term* under each paragraph.

_____ **1**   My husband and I hope to find a house this year. We want to have children, but our apartment is too small. It also doesn't have a yard. We want to have a garden, so we need a big yard. We're going to look for new jobs. We're also going to save our money. When we find our house, we are going to plant a garden. We hope to grow lots of vegetables. After a year, we hope to sell our vegetables at the farmer's market.

short-term / long-term

_____ **2**   My dream is to have my own restaurant in Houston one day. First, I am going to finish my English classes at the community college. Then I am going to apply to the university. I'm going to study business management. I hope to get a scholarship. I hope to have my Bachelor's degree in six years. After that, I intend to work in my uncle's restaurant for a while. Then I am going to apply for a loan and open my restaurant.

short-term / long-term

_____ **3**   One day, I want to be a child-care worker. However, I don't want to do it now. I'm going to wait for my children to get older. When my children are teenagers, I plan to return to school. I'm going to get a certificate as a child-care worker. Then I plan to find a job. After a few more years, I hope to open a day-care center in my house.

short-term / long-term

C Get ideas

Follow these steps to get ideas to write about future plans.

1 Make a list of possible future plans. They can be any future plans: plans for this year, next year, five years from now, or even 40 years from now. Write them in the "Possible Future Plan" column of the chart below.

2 Think about the steps that you are going to take for each plan. Write the steps for each plan in the "Steps" column. Number them.

3 Now think about when each future plan is going to happen. Write a date or a time expression next to each plan in the "When" column. Decide if the plan is short-term or long-term and write "short-term" or "long-term" in the last column.

Possible Future Plan	Steps	When	Short- or Long-term?
travel around Latin America	1 apply for a passport 2 study Spanish 3 save money for trip	in the next two years	short-term

4 Work with a partner. Tell each other about your plans and steps.

5 Did your partner use any words that you can use? Add them to your chart.

D Freewrite

Now it's time to freewrite about your future plans. Describe your plans and the steps for each plan. Are they short- or long-term plans? Write everything that you think of, and don't worry about grammar or spelling. You can write words, phrases, and sentences. Don't stop to erase anything. Just keep writing until your teacher tells you to stop.

A Learn about the simple future with *going to*

> ### *USING* GOING TO
>
> To talk about the future, you can use *be* + *going to* + verb. Use *going to* to talk about plans that are definite.
>
> I **am going to take** classes at the university next year.
>
> He **is going to study** English at the community college for two years.
>
> We **are going to visit** my grandmother next week.
>
> The negative form is *be* + *not* + *going to* + verb.
>
> I**'m not going to get** married for a long time.
>
> You **aren't going to find** a job without a certificate.
>
> She **isn't going to work** in the restaurant after she gets her degree.

Practice 1

Complete the sentences with the correct form of *be* + *going to* + verb. Use the verb in parentheses. Some sentences are negative.

1 We _____ (have) a big family one day.

2 Julien and I hope to get married soon. Then we _____ (move) to New Orleans.

3 Ivan plans to learn to cook well. After that, he _____ (get) a job in a good restaurant.

4 In two years, Junko intends to get pregnant. She _____ (not work) full-time after that.

5 I _____ (save) my money and buy a car next year.

6 I'm going to be very busy at work in the fall, so I _____ (not take) classes in September.

7 My husband and I want to visit Mexico, so we _____ (study) Spanish at the community college this fall.

8 Marisol and Reiko didn't take English 101, so they _____ (not graduate) next year.

Practice 2

Complete this paragraph with *be + going to + verb* or *not be + going to + verb*. Use the verbs below.

apply   be   finish   live   look   move   work

My Nursing Career Plan

I want to be a nurse. First, I _____ my English classes. I
(1)
_____ with my family so I can save money. Then I
(2)
_____ to the nursing program at City College. After I finish
(3)
the nursing program, I _____ for a job. It
(4)
_____ easy to find a job at a hospital, but I hope it doesn't
(5)
take too long. I _____ in the emergency room because it is
(6)
very stressful there. I hope to work with children. After I find a job, my friend
and I _____ into our own apartment.
(7)

B Learn about *plan, expect, intend, hope, want + to + verb*

USING PLAN, EXPECT, INTEND, HOPE, WANT + TO + *VERB*

You can also talk about future plans with *plan, expect, intend, hope, want +
to + verb*.

Plan, expect, intend, hope, and *want* all talk about the future, but these words do
not all mean the same thing.

- Use *plan* and *expect* when you are very sure something is going to happen.
  I **plan to start** classes next semester.
  We **expect to move** to Taiwan in September.

- Use *intend* when you are fairly sure about something but not completely sure.
  They **intend to buy** a new house, but they don't have the money yet.
  She **intends to finish** her degree in four years.

- Use *hope* and *want* to talk about things you want to happen but are less sure
  about. You don't have a definite plan for these things to happen yet.
  Marc **hopes to study** in the United States next year.
  I **want to change** jobs soon.

Practice 3

Make sentences with *plan, expect, intend, hope,* and *want.* Start each sentence with *I plan to, I expect to, I hope to,* etc. Use the words in parentheses to help you to choose the correct verb.

1 get a certificate in Green Gardening (fairly sure)

I intend to get a certificate in Green Gardening.

2 have my own business (less sure)

_____

3 open a Green Gardening business (less sure)

_____

4 work for a gardening business (fairly sure)

_____

5 finish my English studies (very sure)

_____

6 take landscaping classes at a local college (fairly sure)

_____

Practice 4

Put the sentences that you wrote in *Practice 3* into the correct places in the paragraph below. There are different ways to do this. After you finish, compare your paragraphs in small groups.

My Own Business

In five years, _____

_____. First, _____

_____. After that, _____

_____. At the

end of the course, I _____

_____. After

I get my certificate, _____

_____ in my hometown. Finally, when I have enough

experience and enough money, _____

_____.

C Learn about paragraphs

> ### TOPIC SENTENCES
>
> Topic sentences name the topic of the paragraph. They also prepare the reader for the general and specific sentences that follow. In the paragraph below, the topic sentence is the first sentence. It prepares the reader for the sentences that follow about the plan to have a Web design business in 10 years.
>
> #### My Own Web Design Business
>
> <u>In 10 years, I plan to have my own Web design business.</u> First, I plan get a certificate in Web design from City College of San Francisco. I intend to take English classes and business classes for the first year. Then I plan to take graphic design and Web design classes. While I go to school, I plan to get an internship at a Web design company in San Francisco. Then I hope to get a job as a Web designer at one of the Internet design firms in the city. While I work, I plan to save a lot of money. Finally, I hope to open my own Web design business.

Practice 5

Read the paragraph. Then read the sentences below it. Check (✓) any sentence that makes a good topic sentence for the paragraph.

A Trip to Latin America

_____ First, I am going to apply for a passport. I want to talk to the people that I meet, so next semester I'm going to take a Spanish class. Then I intend to save money for the trip. After that, I plan to get Latin American guidebooks at the library and study them. A month before I go, I'm going to make hotel and flight reservations. Finally, I'm going to leave for a great Latin American adventure!

_____ 1 Latin America is an exciting place to visit.

_____ 2 I plan to travel around Latin America some day.

_____ 3 Colombia is in Latin America.

_____ 4 There are many interesting sights in Latin America.

_____ 5 In the next few years, I'm going to visit Latin America.

Your turn ↰

Look back at your Freewrite. Choose one plan to write about. On a piece of paper, write a topic sentence.

D Write the first draft

Now it's time to write the first draft. Write about your future plans. Use your freewrite, your *Your turn* notes, and your ideas and language from Sections I and II to help you. You can also add any other ideas that come to mind.

III REVISING YOUR WRITING

A Expand your vocabulary

> ### *FUTURE TIME EXPRESSIONS*
>
> You can use future time expressions to talk about when something is going to happen.
>
> These expressions describe a specific or definite time in the future.
>
> | | | | |
> |---|---|---|---|
> | tomorrow | next week | next month | next year |
> | in X days | in X weeks | in X months | in X years |
>
> These words and phrases describe more general times or an indefinite time in the future.
>
> | | | | |
> |---|---|---|---|
> | soon | one day | in the future | later on |
>
> Remember to use a comma if you put the time expression at the beginning of the sentence.
>
> **In five years,** I plan to have my own business.
>
> **One day,** I hope to travel around the world.

Practice 6

Lucia is a 20-year old college student. Read about her plans. Some are definite and some are not definite. On a separate piece of paper, write a sentence about each plan. Use a time expression from the box above.

Definite	Not Definite
Get a business degree at the university	Get promoted at my job
Move to New York	Have a house with a big yard and three children
Apply for a job at a small business in New York	Travel around Asia

Your turn ↩

Look at your first draft. Add at least two sentences with future time expressions. Remember to mark where these sentences go.

B Connect your ideas

> ### ORDERING WORDS
>
> Ordering words tell the order in which things happen. Here are some common ordering words.
>
> first   second   then   next   finally
>
> Use a comma after all ordering words except *then*.
>
> > **First,** I'm going to finish my degree. **Then** I'm going to apply for a passport. **Next,** I plan to apply to graduate school in Australia. I want to study the Great Barrier Reef and the animals that live there. **Finally,** I hope to move to Darwin. It's a fascinating city.
>
> Note: Don't overuse ordering words. Not every sentence in your paragraph needs an ordering word.

Practice 7

Complete the paragraphs with ordering words from the box above.

Paragraph 1

> I want to move to Seattle next year. _____ (1), I plan to do research on jobs in the city. I hope to find a job in a hospital because I am a nurse. _____ (2) I'm going to find out about apartments. I hope they don't cost too much. Just in case, I plan to save a lot of money before I move. _____ (3), I'm going to sell my car because you don't really need a car in Seattle.

Paragraph 2

> One day, I hope to become a private chef. _____ (1), I am going to apply to cooking school. I hope to get a degree in culinary arts. _____ (2), I intend to get a job at a restaurant in town because I want to get some work experience. _____ (3) I'm going to apply for jobs in all the big hotels because I want to learn how to make very fancy dishes. _____ (4), I intend to apply for private chef jobs in Dallas because there are a lot of opportunities for private chefs there.

Your turn ↶

Look at your first draft. Add at least two sentences with ordering words. Remember to mark where these sentences go.

C Give and get feedback

Work with a partner. Follow these steps to get feedback on your writing.

1 Show your partner your first draft with the sentences you added to it.
2 Exchange books. Answer the questions in the chart below about your partner's first draft.

	Your Partner's Writing
How many words from the *Vocabulary Pool* did your partner use?	
How many sentences with *be going to* are there?	
How many sentences with *plan, expect, intend, hope,* and *want to* are there?	
Are there any sentences that aren't about both the topic and the topic sentence? If yes, how many?	
How many sentences with future time expressions are there?	
How many sentences with ordering words are there?	

3 What do you like about your partner's piece of writing? Underline two or three parts. Tell your partner.
4 Show your partner the chart. Discuss your answers. Do you have any suggestions for your partner?
5 Return your partner's book.

D Write the second draft

Follow these steps to write the second draft.

1 Look at the chart your partner completed for your first draft. Think about what your partner said. Did your partner give you any ideas you can use? For example, can you add any more sentences with ordering words?
2 Check that all sentences are about both the topic and the topic sentence.
3 Look at the *Progress Check* on page 144 of Chapter 9. Use it to help you revise your first draft.
4 Rewrite your paragraph with the changes.

A Focus on mechanics

> **WRITING TITLES**
>
> Use the topic of your paragraph to create a title. Titles should be interesting. They should also let the reader know what to expect in the paragraph. Look at these titles for a paragraph about a plan to become a chef.
>
> Becoming a Private Chef
>
> From the Classroom to the Kitchen
>
> My Plan to Become a Private Chef
>
> Two Years to Become a Chef
>
> The first word in a title always starts with a capital letter. Most of the other words start with capital letters, too. However, articles (*a*, *an*, and *the*), short prepositions (*to*, *at*, and *in*), and conjunctions (*and*, *or*) do not start with a capital letter. Center your title above the first line of your paragraph.

Practice 8

Rewrite the titles using correct capital letters.

1 hopes and dreams for a nurse _____

2 my plan for my family _____

3 saving money for a house _____

4 getting a job teaching young children _____

5 a trip to costa rica next summer _____

Practice 9

Read the paragraph. Underline the topic sentence. Then circle the best title on page 157.

> I hope to work in many countries for the next 10 years. First, I plan to get a job as an engineer with an international company. After a while, I hope to go to another country to work with that company. I want to go to the Middle East to work. There are a lot of jobs there for engineers. Also, I like hot weather, and it is hot there. I'm going to study Arabic before I go. Next, I want to work in Thailand. Thailand is a very beautiful country. Finally, I want to work in Singapore or Hong Kong. I hope to save a lot of money in those jobs. When I return to South Korea, I hope to get a job managing engineering projects.

a Returning to South Korea after Ten Years
b Working as an Engineer
c Working Overseas as an Engineer

Practice 10

Reread the two paragraphs in *Practice 7*. With a partner, write a title for each paragraph.

Paragraph 1: _____

Paragraph 2: _____

Your turn ↶

Look at your second draft. Write a title for your paragraph.

B Check for common mistakes

> ### FORMING THE FUTURE WITH VERB + TO
>
> Many students make mistakes with the future with *be going, plan, expect, intend, hope,* and *want* + *to* + verb.
>
> - Remember to use *to*.
>   I hope ∧ get married one day. *(to)*
>
> - Remember to use the verb in its base form after *to*.
>   He plans to ~~moves~~ into an apartment with me. *(move)*
>
> - Remember to use *be* with *going to*.
>   One day, I going to go to Europe. *(I'm)*
>
> - Remember to use the correct form of *be*.
>   Our children ~~is~~ going to start a business together. *(are)*
>
> - Remember to use the *-ing* form of *going to*.
>   I'm ~~go~~ to get a job in a restaurant. *(going)*

Practice **11**

Read this paragraph. Find eight more mistakes. Write the corrections above them.

Having a Family

¹In two years, my boyfriend and I ~~am~~ *are* going to get married. ²We want to finish school first. ³I expect finish school in two years, but my boyfriend plans to finishes next year. ⁴Then we intend look for jobs. ⁵We hope to find jobs in Tokyo. ⁶We going to look for jobs in the same area. ⁷After that, we are going look for an apartment. ⁸We both want live close to our work. ⁹Finally, we are go to get married. ¹⁰We hope to have our wedding in Hawaii. ¹¹We want to having a beautiful wedding!

C Edit your writing

Use the *Editing Checklist* below to edit your paragraph. Look for only one kind of mistake each time you read your sentences. For example, the first time you read your sentences, ask yourself, "Does every sentence start with a capital letter?"

EDITING CHECKLIST ☑

☐ **1** Does every sentence start with a capital letter?

☐ **2** Does every sentence end with a period?

☐ **3** Did you spell all your words correctly?

☐ **4** Did you indent the first line of your paragraph?

☐ **5** Did you use *be going, plan, expect, intend, hope,* and *want* + *to* + verb correctly?

☐ **6** Did you use commas after future time expressions that come at the beginning of a sentence?

D Write the final draft

Make all your changes on your second draft. Remember to mark where the changes go. This time, type your paragraph on a computer. Make any changes that you need.

A Share your writing

Follow these steps to share your writing.

1 On a computer, copy and paste your paragraph onto a new page.
   - Put each sentence of your paragraph on a separate line with four spaces between each sentence.
   - Print your list of sentences.
   - Cut each sentence into strips of paper so that each strip of paper has only one sentence on it.
2 In class, put the sentences on your desk and jumble them so they are not in order.
3 Change desks with a partner and:
   - Find the topic sentence.
   - Put the other sentences in order.
   - Look at each other's new paragraphs to see if they are correct.
4 Jumble the sentences again and repeat the process with another partner.

B Check your progress

After you get your writing back from your teacher, complete the *Progress Check* below.

PROGRESS CHECK

Date: _____

New vocabulary I used: _____

_____

_____

New grammar I used: _____

_____

New paragraph skills I learned: _____

_____

Connecting words I used: _____

Mechanics I learned: _____

Things I need to remember the next time I write: _____

_____

Appendix

A Country, nationality, and language words

Country	Nationality	Language
Argentina	Argentinean	Spanish
Australia	Australian	English
Brazil	Brazilian	Portuguese
Canada	Canadian	English / French
Chile	Chilean	Spanish
China	Chinese	Mandarin Chinese / Cantonese
Colombia	Colombian	Spanish
Egypt	Egyptian	Arabic
France	French	French
Great Britain	British	English
Indonesia	Indonesian	Indonesian
Iraq	Iraqi	Arabic / Kurdish
Israel	Israeli	Hebrew
Italy	Italian	Italian
Japan	Japanese	Japanese
Mexico	Mexican	Spanish
the Philippines	Philippine / Filipino	Tagalog / English
Russia	Russian	Russian
Saudi Arabia	Saudi Arabian	Arabic
South Korea	South Korean	Korean
Spain	Spanish	Spanish
Thailand	Thai	Thai
Turkey	Turkish	Turkish
the United States	American	English
Vietnam	Vietnamese	Vietnamese

B Capitalization

1 What do I *capitalize*?

a The first word in every sentence:		The yard has trees and flowers. We went to several museums.
b The pronoun *I*:	My sister and I went to the same college. I think that I will stay home tonight.	
c Names:	Mariella Henandez, Martin M. Smith	
d Days:	Sunday, Monday, Tuesday, Wednesday, Thursday, Friday, Saturday, Sunday	
e Months:	January, February, March, April, May, June, July, August, September, October, November, December	
f Holidays:	Valentine's Day, New Year's Day	
g Nationalities:	Korean, Thai, Mexican	
h Languages:	Chinese, English, Arabic	
i Cities:	New York, Jakarta, Tokyo	
j Countries:	Canada, Brazil, Australia	
k Continents:	South America, Africa, Europe	

2 What do I *not capitalize*?

a Seasons:	spring, summer, winter, fall (autumn)
b Sports:	basketball, tennis, football
c School subjects:	mathematics, biology, history

C Spelling rules (1)

The following are spelling rules for:

- Changing the endings of simple present verbs when the subject of the verb is a singular noun or *he*, *she*, or *it*
- Changing the endings of singular count nouns to make plural nouns

---

a For most words, add only *-s*. This is also the rule for words ending in *-e*.

run – run**s**
dance – dance**s**
school – school**s**

b For words that end in *-s*, *-ss*, *-sh*, *-ch*, or *-x*, add *-es*.

bus – bus**es**
kiss – kiss**es**
brush – brush**es**
watch – watch**es**
box – box**es**

c For words that end with a vowel (*a*, *e*, *i*, *o*, *u*) + *-y*, add only *-s*.

toy – toy**s**
buy – buy**s**
day – day**s**

d For words that end with a consonant (all other letters) + *-y*, change the *-y* to *-i* and add *-es*.

study – stud**ies**
fly – fl**ies**

D Common irregular verbs

Base form	Past	Base form	Past
be	was, were	hold	held
beat	beat	hurt	hurt
become	became	keep	kept
begin	began	know	knew
bend	bent	leave	left
bet	bet	let	let
bite	bit	lose	lost
bleed	bled	make	made
blow	blew	meet	met
break	broke	pay	paid
bring	brought	read	read
build	built	ride	rode
buy	bought	ring	rang
catch	caught	run	ran
choose	chose	say	said
come	came	see	saw
cost	cost	sell	sold
cut	cut	send	sent
dig	dug	shake	shook
do	did	show	showed
draw	drew	shut	shut
drink	drank	sing	sang
drive	drove	sit	sat
eat	ate	spend	spent
fight	fought	stand	stood
find	found	steal	stole
fly	flew	swim	swam
forget	forgot	take	took
forgive	forgave	teach	taught
freeze	froze	tell	told
get	got	think	thought
give	gave	throw	threw
go	went	understand	understood
have, has	had	wake	woke
hear	heard	wear	wore
hide	hid	win	won
hit	hit	write	wrote

E Common non-count nouns

advice	music
air	
art	news
baggage	paper
bread	pasta
	peace
coffee	pepper
	progress
English	
equipment	rain
	research
fog	running
food	
freedom	safety
friendship	salt
furniture	sand
	science
garbage	snow
	soccer
happiness	swimming
homework	
honesty	tea
housework	tennis
	time
information	traffic
	transportation
knowledge	travel
laundry	vocabulary
love	
luck	water
luggage	weather
	wind
math	wood
money	work

F Spelling rules (2)

The following are spelling rules for changing the endings of regular verbs to form the simple past tense.

---

a For verbs that end in -*e*, add only -*d*.

smile – smile**d**
hope – hope**d**

b Verbs ending in -*y*

- When there is a vowel (*a, e, i, o, u*) before the -*y*, keep the -*y* and add -*ed*.

stay – stay**ed**
enjoy – enjoy**ed**

- When there is a consonant (all other letters) before the -*y*, change the -*y* to -*i* and add -*ed*.

cry – cr**ied**
hurry – hurr**ied**

c Verbs ending in a consonant

- For verbs that end in two consonants, add -*ed*.

tal<u>k</u> – talk**ed**
  cc

hel<u>p</u> – help**ed**
  cc

- For verbs that end in two vowels and a consonant, add -*ed*.

w<u>ait</u> – wait**ed**
  vvc

p<u>our</u> – pour**ed**
  vvc

- For verbs that end in a consonant, a vowel, and another consonant, double the end consonant and add -*ed*.

<u>hop</u> – hop**ped**
 cvc

<u>step</u> – step**ped**
 cvc

- Note these exceptions.

listen – listen**ed**
offer – offer**ed**

- Do not double *w* or *x*.

snow – snow**ed**
mix – mix**ed**
